THE FINANCIAL REPORTING

PROJECT AND READINGS 4e

CLAYTON A. HOCK
Miami University

BRUCE A. BALDWIN
Arizona State University West

THOMSON
™
SOUTH-WESTERN

Australia · Canada · Mexico · Singapore · Spain · United Kingdom · United States

THOMSON

SOUTH-WESTERN

The Financial Reporting Project and Readings, 4e

Clayton A. Hock and Bruce A. Baldwin

VP/Editorial Director:
Jack W. Calhoun

Acquisitions Editor:
Julie Moulton

Marketing Manager:
Keith Chasse

Editorial Assistant:
Allison Rolfes

Production Editor:
Amy McGuire

Technology Project Editor:
Robin Browning

Manufacturing Coordinator:
Doug Wilke

Printer:
Globus Printing, Inc.
Minster, Ohio

Art Director:
Tippy McIntosh

Cover Designer:
Justin Klefeker

Cover Image:
© PhotoDisc

Table of Contents

Item	Title	Page

Preface to the Student

The primary purpose of the **Financial Reporting Project** (**FRP**) is for you to experience up-to-date *live* financial statements *in their natural habitat*. For most users of financial statements, the natural habitat is the Annual Report to Stockholders or the Securities and Exchange Commission (SEC) Form 10-K Report. While portions of real financial statements may be illustrated in your textbook, this project will *put it all together*. You will work with the complete and integrated financial reports of a live company as you apply the lessons of your accounting course. The development and application of this accounting knowledge will advance your career.

Be aware that, occasionally, some of the ratio formulas you use in this project are slightly different from the basic ratio formulas used in your textbook. This is necessary because of the more complex data you will sometimes encounter in complete sets of live financial statements. When learning the basic formulas in a textbook setting, it is much easier for you to learn the underlying concepts if complicating factors are assumed away. When dealing with live data, however, you must be able to incorporate the complexities or you risk arriving at an inappropriate conclusion. Part of the purpose of the **FRP** is to help you make that transition. When these slight modifications are introduced, the circumstances necessitating them are explained. The good news is that these modifications are usually very minor.

Another purpose of the **FRP** is to familiarize you with common sources of business and financial information. Employers expect that you are able to quickly and accurately obtain business and financial information about suppliers, customers, or competitors. Many of the assignments in this project will require you to use classic reference sources from the library or Internet that are used every day in the business world.

A third purpose of the **FRP** is to build teamwork skills. Many employers have made the remark, "You professors educate students one-at-a-time, but we employers work them in teams." Today, employers expect that you will have experience working closely on team-oriented projects. You may already know that teamwork skills take time and effort to develop. This is all part of your education, and failure to develop and extend your teamwork skills is just as dangerous to your career as failing to master personal computer and communication skills.

A fourth purpose of the **FRP** is to develop your writing skills, which is important for success in the business world. Depending on your professor's instructions, and based on your understanding and analysis of the material found in your annual report, you may prepare one of two written assignments:
(1) write one longer paper at the end of the **FRP**—Assignment 13; or
(2) write a series of up to five short memos (one to three pages, or a length set by your professor) as you complete Assignments 4, 7, 10, 12 and 13.

Preface to the Professor

The **FRP** has been used successfully in the sophomore-level introductory accounting course and in the MBA financial accounting course. As in the Third Edition, Internet web sites have been integrated into the assignments. Where appropriate, students are guided to the **Financial Reporting Project** (**FRP**) homepage at **hock.swlearning.com**. After selecting "assignments" the students can obtain relevant hot links to free web sites. All assignments, however, can still be completed using only traditional library resources.

This project is the result of many years of experimentation with students—that they successfully make the transition from classroom topics and textbook examples to the use and understanding of *real* financial statements. The **FRP** (which includes analysis of the SEC 10-K and the proxy statement) is designed to achieve this. An unanticipated side benefit of this project has been that students enjoy dealing with *live* financial information. It's often amazing how students will pore over the annual reports, proxy statements and SEC 10-Ks that they have received in the mail or downloaded from the Internet. When they run into complicated issues, their curiosity is piqued and they want to know more. Students are also intrigued by current readings. Each reading introduces an issue or issues related to the corresponding assignment.

Student Teams. While this project is a valuable tool when completed by students working individually, its learning benefits are maximized when it is completed by student teams. The strategy is to assign a different company to each team in the class. Each student obtains his/her own copies of the annual report, 10-K and proxy statement. The assigned company can then be used for a variety of in-class and out-of-class team-based assignments. Each team member is expected to become an expert regarding his/her company and then contribute that knowledge to a written report prepared by the team. Teams can also make end-of-semester class presentations based on their written report. See the *Manual* for guidelines about teams.

Assignment Options. Like the previous edition of the **FRP**, this one provides an alternative to the Capstone Project in Assignment 13—a series of up to five short memos as part of Assignments 4, 7, 10, 12, and 13.

Other assignments ask the students to compare answers regarding their company with classmates. As an alternative, they may obtain the same information from other annual reports found on the Internet. Both options are discussed in more detail in the *Instructor's Manual.*

The *Instructor's Manual* provides a master list of The Dow30 companies, the NASDAQ 100, and the NYSE U.S. 100 Index. Each company is identified by name and ticker symbol. The *Instructor's Manual* also provides a variety of hints and suggestions regarding use of the **FRP** (e.g., suggested guidelines about forming teams).

From the Authors. Thanks to many persons for their assistance in bringing this project to fruition. Students, for example, provided many helpful criticisms of early versions of many assignments. Faculty colleagues did the same. Special thanks to Ethel Hock for formatting this Fourth Edition and preparing the camera-ready copy. Special thanks also to Susan Hurst, Miami University Business Librarian, who updated the resource references and the accompanying web site. All errors and omissions, however, are our personal responsibility.

We hope that you find this project helpful and useful. If you have suggestions for improvement, please call, write, or send e-mail. Your suggestions are welcome.

Clayton A. Hock
Department of Accountancy
Miami University
317-D Laws Hall
Oxford, OH   45056-1602

Phone: 513-529-6246
Fax: 513-529-4740
E-mail: hockca@muohio.edu

Bruce A. Baldwin
School of Management
Arizona State University West
P.O. Box 37100
Phoenix, Arizona   85069-7100

Phone: 602-543-6210
Fax: 602-543-6303
E-mail: bruce.baldwin@asu.edu

Introduction to Memos

Memos are a primary and effective means of communication within an organization. Generally, they are brief and to the point as busy executives do not have time to wade through long and rambling reports. Typically, memos have a beginning similar to the one illustrated below, which appears in the upper left-hand corner. Further, headings are often used to allow the reader to quickly determine the major points.

Date memo is written.

To: Person(s) to whom the memo is addressed.
From: The person(s) writing the memo.
Subject: The purpose of the memo.

Note

Further discussion about writing memos can be found in Chapter 5 of *Essentials of Business Communications*, Sixth Edition, by Mary Ellen Guffey, South-Western, 2004.

Based on different aspects of your **FRP** company, you will form opinions about the company which you may express in the form of a memo after Assignments 4, 7, 10, 12 and 13. Each memo is described in a double-lined box on the last page of these assignments. To maintain a focus to your memos, the following scenario is provided, although your professor may develop another basis for the memos.

> You or your team are starting a firm to advise investors. A potential client has asked that you assist her in evaluating a company (your selected **FRP** company) which she might add to her investment portfolio. Also, based on the usefulness and quality of your memos and advice, she will determine whether or not to stay with your firm.

Each memo is another step in the development of your final memo after Assignment 13, which will culminate your research.

Assignment 1
Choosing a Company and
Securing Its Annual Report

The purpose of the **Financial Reporting Project** (**FRP**) is to apply the lessons of your accounting course to a real company. You will discover how the issues, topics, practices and procedures described in your textbook actually affect a company's financial statements. You will conduct library and/or Internet research to familiarize yourself with your company and the industry in which your firm competes. Later in the course you will begin to analyze and evaluate your individual firm's financial stability and trends.

Your company may be assigned to you by your professor or your professor may allow you to choose your own company. However your company is chosen, it will be the basis for this FRP.

The company should be publically traded, i.e., its stock is traded on a stock exchange such as the New York Stock Exchange (NYSE). It is usually best to avoid financial institutions, e.g., banks or insurance companies, as well as public utilities, because these companies normally have specialized accounting practices. Your professor may give you additional guidelines on choosing a company.

Identifying Companies from Which to Choose

Recognizing that your professor may have placed some limitations on your choice, here are some ways to identify possible companies.

1. You might want to select an industry that interests you for one of many reasons:

    a. Someone you know works in that industry or you have worked in a particular industry about which you would like to learn more.

    b. A company in that industry is located in your hometown or in a nearby location.

    c. You regularly purchase products from that industry (e.g., textbooks, clothing, or beverages).

    d. The industry might provide employment opportunities after graduation.

    e. The industry has been in the news lately, and you are interested in being better informed about the issues that were raised.

2. A good place to start is in your school's library. Following are five sources that provide information about many industries and specific information about individual firms in those industries.

a. *Standard & Poor's Industry Surveys*, published by Standard & Poor's, Inc. This three-volume document is published every quarter and updated twice a year. It covers approximately 52 industries and more than 1,200 companies. In the front of each volume you will find a section entitled the "Index to Companies." This section lists all of the industry categories and each of the companies within each industry.

b. *Value Line Investment Survey*, published by Value Line, Inc. This service is updated weekly and comes in three parts. The front page of Part 1, "Summary & Index," lists more than 90 industry categories along with the page number where information on each industry can be found. In Part 3 you will find the industry information as well as specific information about each company in each industry.

c. *Fortune* is a bi-weekly business magazine published by AOL Time Warner. Its annual mid-April listing of the 500 largest firms in the United States is referred to as the Fortune 500 and is probably the most widely cited listing of this type.

d. *Hoover's Handbook of American Business*, published by Hoover's, Inc., profiles 750 major U.S. companies, including overview, history, officers, location, products, and competitors.

e. The *North American Industry Classification System* (NAICS, pronounced "nakes") was developed by the U.S., Canada and Mexico after the North American Free Trade Agreement (NAFTA). Published by the U.S. Government Office of Management & Budget, the NAICS replaced SIC codes (Standard Industrial Classification) set up in the 1930s. The NAICS reclassifies industries to better reflect the North American economy, now more service oriented and technological than manufacturing based.

Use the NAICS manual to select an industry and its six-digit NAICS code. Then go to the *D & B Million Dollar Directory* published by Dun & Bradstreet, Inc. This directory is a series of five volumes; look for the one labeled "Series Cross-Reference by Industry." This volume is organized by NAICS code numbers. You will find many companies for whatever NAICS code you have chosen along with each firm's mailing address and telephone number.

On the Internet

The Internet is a rich source of financial information and there are references throughout this book to many helpful sites. Convenient access is also provided through the Ingram homepage.

Go to **hock.swlearning.com**, select "assignments," and explore the hot links listed under Assignment 1.

More information about the NAICS can be found on the NAICS Association web site at **www.naics.com**.

Group Project

(If you are not part of a group, skip down to Obtaining Financial Statements.)

If your group is to evaluate several firms in the same industry, your first task will be to assign a specific company to each member of your group. This will be your first exercise in group decision making.

Each group member is expected to become very knowledgeable regarding one or all of your team's assigned companies. You will obtain the company's financial statements and observe how your firm implements the principles and practices that you will learn in this course. If team members have been assigned a different firm, the other members of your group will be doing the same thing for their firms (which compete with yours).

Each member will contribute his/her expertise regarding the assigned firm(s) to the group's report, which will be due on a date announced by your professor. If your professor requires you to complete Assignment 13, there are more instructions on the group report and analysis in that Assignment.

You should review those instructions *very soon* and begin to develop strategies for completion of the project.

First, however, complete the following steps.

1. Choose a name for your group and write it in the space below. Feel free to be creative. For example, you might want to select a name that is a clever play-on-words regarding the name of your company or industry. Your professor will probably appreciate the humor.

   Group name _____

2. List each person in your group with telephone number and e-mail address.

Group Member Names	Phone Numbers	E-mail Addresses
a. _____	_____	_____
b. _____	_____	_____
c. _____	_____	_____
d. _____	_____	_____
e. _____	_____	_____
f. _____	_____	_____

3. Turn in one copy of the group information to your professor.

Obtaining Financial Statements

Most future assignments will be based on information contained in your company's Annual Report, its SEC Form 10-K, and its proxy statement. You will need to secure the most recent copy of the these items.

The Annual Report is a document that must be distributed to all shareholders every year. It contains the firm's financial statements as well as a variety of other required and optional information. Often it is a slick and glossy publication with color pictures of the executives, company facilities, and products. The SEC Form 10-K is the version of the annual report that must be filed annually with the Securities and Exchange Commission (SEC), an agency of the federal government in Washington, D.C. When you secure your firm's Annual Report and SEC 10-K you will notice that the two documents have many similarities but that they also have some striking differences.

The proxy statement is a document describing matters that will be discussed or voted on at the annual stockholders' meeting. It is also the device by which management of the corporation solicits your authorization (proxy) to vote your shares on its behalf. Of greatest interest, perhaps, is that proxy statements must provide detailed information about compensation of key executive personnel. (Ever wonder how much money the president of a large corporation is paid?)

Obtaining the Required Materials from the Company

1. Contact your company directly by telephone, letter, or e-mail. You will need to go to your university library, community public library, or the Internet to obtain this information. The address, and usually the phone number, can be obtained from the following sources:

   a. *LexisNexis Corporate Affiliations*, LexisNexis Group.

   b. *D&B Million Dollar Directory*, Dun & Bradstreet.

   c. *Mergent Industrial Manual*, Mergent, Inc.

   d. *Hoover's Handbook of American Business*, Hoover's, Inc.

   e. The company's web site, usually the company's name followed by ".com." Once at the company's homepage, click under a heading such as *Investor Services* or *Investor Relations*.

   > ## On the Internet
   > Web sites at which you may learn how to contact your company are listed on the Ingram homepage.
   >
   > Go to **hock.swlearning.com**, select "assignments," and explore the hot links under Assignment 1.

2. The following hints will help you secure the necessary materials.

   a. Companies usually have an Office of Investor Relations or Shareholder Relations. Write to, or telephone, that office. If your company has an Internet homepage, you may be able to send an e-mail request directly.

b. Explain that you are a student at (identify your school) and that as part of an accounting class assignment this term you will be studying the firm and its financial information.

c. Request a copy of the firm's most recent Annual Report, most recent SEC Form 10-K, and its most recent proxy statement. Most firms are happy to provide these documents. They tend to think of you either as a potential investor, potential customer, or both.

d. Provide an *exact* mailing address.

3. Note the following information regarding your request.

a. Method of making the request (e.g., telephone, fax, letter, e-mail)

_____

b. Post office address or e-mail address of firm (if you sent a letter or e-mail)

_____

_____

_____

c. Phone number of firm (if you telephoned or faxed) _____

d. Date of request for documents _____

Obtaining the Required Materials from the Company's Web site

Though having a real "glossy" annual report and proxy statement would be preferable, it is not always possible to get one in a timely manner. Therefore, you may want to consider securing your company's annual report and proxy from the Internet.

When obtaining your annual report from your company's web site, it is not necessary to download and print the entire report, which can reach nearly 100 pages in length. Since only a portion of the annual report will be used consistently, it is suggested that you print only the following: (1) Management Discussion and Analysis (MD&A), (2) financial statement, and (3) notes to financial statements. During the FRP the other sections of the annual report will be referred to only once or twice or not at all. Any information needed from these sections can be secured by scrolling through the annual report.

Sample Letter

If you prefer to write a letter it could be similar to the one on the following page.

Later Assignments

In later assignments you will compare information about your company with information from the annual reports of your classmates or from annual reports found on the Internet.

Sample Letter

(Your Name and Address)

(Today's Date)

Investor Relations Department
Humble Pie Bakery Corporation
3652 Modesty Boulevard
Ovenhot, Arizona 00000

Director of Investor Relations:

I am a student at (name your school). As part of an accounting
class assignment this term I will be examining and analyzing the
financial reports of a major corporation.

I have chosen your firm and would like to study the financial
reports of your corporation as part of my class assignment. Would
you please assist me by sending me a copy of your most recent
Annual Report, most recent SEC 10-K, and most recent Proxy
Statement? Thank you very much for your help!

Sincerely,

(Signature)

(Your Name, typed)

Name _____   Professor _____

Course _____   Section _____

Completing Assignment 1 – Choosing a Company

1. What is the name of the company you have chosen?

   _____

2. Which industry category does your firm represent?

   _____

3. Write several paragraphs describing how (and why) you chose the firm you did. Did you use any of the resources listed earlier in this assignment, or the Internet? Were they easy to use? Hard to use? Which one(s) would you recommend to friends if they had to complete this assignment? Discuss.

   Note: *Please think and plan carefully before writing. Readability, spelling, organization, grammar, and sentence structure will all be considered in grading your response.*

   _____
   _____
   _____
   _____
   _____
   _____
   _____
   _____
   _____
   _____
   _____
   _____
   _____
   _____
   _____
   _____
   _____
   _____

Assignment 2
Understanding Your Company and Its Environment

A company's financial statements are best understood when the reader understands the company and comprehends fully the environment in which the firm operates: economic, social, legal and political. The purpose of this assignment is to gain an understanding of selected factual aspects of your company. You will read an article about your company, which may reveal a shakeup of key management personnel or new product development, and read an article about your company's current environment. There may be important new legislation that has affected your firm. Additionally, new technology, new competitors, new social trends, or legal battles could all affect the general health of your firm.

Key References for this Assignment

The following are excellent sources of background information on companies and/or industries. If some of the suggested references are not available in your library, your reference librarian may be able to suggest other sources that you could use instead. In addition, almost every industry has a periodical, such as *Progressive Grocer* or *Advertising Age*, which would be a good source of information about issues facing the industry.

1. *Standard & Poor's Industry Surveys*, published by Standard & Poor's, Inc. This three-volume document is published every quarter and updated twice a year. It covers approximately 52 industries and more than 1,200 companies.

2. *Value Line Investment Survey*, published by Value Line, Inc. This weekly service is comprised of three sections. The "Summary and Index" (Part 1) lists the page numbers in Part 3 where information regarding your industry category can be found. The *Value Line Investment Survey* provides detailed reports on approximately 1,700 companies across more than 90 industry groups.

3. *Manufacturing & Distribution USA*, published by Gale Research. This three volume set is an excellent comprehensive guide to economic activity in manufacturing industries, including analyses, statistics, and leading companies.

4. *Encyclopedia of American Industries*, published by Gale Research. Provides detailed, comprehensive information on a wide range of industries in every realm of American business.

5. *Ward's Business Directory of U.S. Private and Public Companies*, published by Gale Research.

6. *Mergent Industry Review*, published by Mergent FIS. Identifies and compares companies within industries.

7. *Standard & Poor's Register of Corporations, Directors and Executives*, published by Standard & Poor's (S&P). This three volume set covers over 75,000 corporations and profiles 350,000 executives.

8. *Standard Corporate Descriptions*, published by Standard & Poor's. Information on US and international companies includes full income statements and balance sheets, extensive corporate profiles, and recent news.

9. *Standard & Poor's 500 Guide*, published by Standard & Poor's. Corporate information and financial statement statistics are provided by the components of the S&P 500 Index.

10. *LexisNexis Corporate Affiliations*, published by the LexisNexis Group. Public, private and international companies in two volumes (A - L and M - Z), which contain detailed information about each company.

11. *America's Corporate Families*, published by Dun & Bradstreet, Inc. Volume I provides detailed information on all "ultimate" parent companies. Volume II cross-references the "ultimate" parent company and its subsidiaries.

12. *Business Newsbank*, Newsbank, Inc.

13. *Business Periodicals Index*, H.W. Wilson Company

14. *The New York Times Index*, New York Times Company

15. *The Wall Street Journal Index*, Dow-Jones & Company

On the Internet

Alternatively, or in addition to your library search, you may want to "surf the net" for trends and developments affecting your company's industry. This will be easier if you know the company's stock ticker symbol, a one-to-five letter code under which the company's stock trades on the stock exchange. If you don't already know the ticker symbol, go to the Ingram homepage at **hock.swlearning.com**, select "assignments," and explore the hot links listed under Assignment 2.

Note

Web sites appear or disappear suddenly. Sometimes data that *was* free suddenly requires a fee.

Name _____   Professor _____

Course _____   Section _____

Completing Assignment 2 – Understanding Your Company

1. Use the Key References listed on pages 9 and 10 or the Internet to obtain the information requested below and to answer the questions that follow. Most companies' web sites are the "company name.com," e.g., Staples is staples.com and Coca-cola is cocacola.com. The Web site can also be found through a search engine such as Google.

    Note: *Please think and plan carefully before answering the questions. Readability, organization, spelling, grammar, and sentence structure will all be considered in grading your responses.*

    a. Basic company facts:

    Complete name of firm _____

    Stock ticker symbol _____

    Stock exchange where traded _____

    Primary and secondary NAICS codes (or SIC) _____

    State of incorporation _____

    Year of incorporation _____

    Independent auditor _____

    Company's fiscal year-end (month and day) _____

    Web site _____

    b. List up to five products your company produces (manufacturing company) or sells (retailing company) and customers to whom those products are probably sold.

    Product   Customer

    _____   _____

    _____   _____

    _____   _____

    _____   _____

    _____   _____

    c. The size of a company is determined by more than one factor. For those factors listed, enter the amount or number for your company.

    Note: *For a better analysis of your company's size, it would be best to compare your company's numbers with the industry average, if available.*

11

Dollar amount of assets   _____

Dollar amount of sales/revenues   _____

Net income   _____

Number of products/services   _____

Earnings per share (diluted)   _____

Number of common shares outstanding   _____

Other measures:

_____

_____

Based on the numbers listed above, would your company be classified as large? Briefly discuss.

_____

_____

_____

_____

_____

_____

_____

_____

d. Each public company is required to have a Board of Directors (BD) and often there is a picture of the BD near the end of the annual report. Relative to your company's BD, complete the following:

Total number of individuals serving on the BD: _____

Composition of BD by gender: male _____   female _____

Composition of BD by ethnic group: African American _____

    Asian _____   Caucasian _____   Other _____

How many members are "independent," i.e., have no official relationship/ position with the company? _____

How many members are "insiders," i.e., hold a position within the company, e.g., treasurer? _____

Would you say that your company's BD is diversified? Why?

_____

_____

_____

How would describe the average age of the BD? _____

_____

_____

2. Use the Key References listed on pages 9 and 10 to identify two articles (no more than two years old), one about your firm and another about its industry. If they convey significant or interesting information, photocopy (or download and print) them to turn in with this assignment. Only one article may be from the Internet.

    Note: *It is a serious breach of academic integrity to tear articles out of magazines that do not belong to you, e.g., those in the library. Please don't do it!*

    a. The first article looks at your company. Various facts, allegations, successes and failures about a company are often the focus of articles in the business and popular press. These articles should be more objective and provide a perspective other than management's point of view.

    Search method

    Key Reference _____ Edition _____

    Web site _____

    Author _____

    Title _____

    Name of periodical or Web site _____

    Date of periodical _____

    Page numbers (Normally not available on an Internet source) _____

    Describe why this article is significant and interesting. Limit your response to no more than 100 words and use complete sentences.

    _____

    _____

    _____

    _____

    _____

    _____

    _____

    _____

    _____

    _____

    _____

    _____

    _____

b. To further your understanding of your company, the second article focuses on the industry of which your firm is a part. Overall trends within an industry generally have a large impact on the success of specific firms within the industry. Through your search process, you will gain some insight into the nature of the industry in which your firm competes.

Search method

   Key Reference _____ Edition _____

   Web site _____

Author _____

Title _____

Name of periodical or Web site _____

Date of periodical _____

Page numbers (Normally not available on an Internet source) _____

Describe why this article is significant and interesting. Limit your response to no more than 100 words and use complete sentences.

_____

_____

_____

_____

_____

_____

_____

_____

_____

_____

_____

_____

_____

3. What are the two most interesting aspects of your company (or its industry) that you have discovered so far? Briefly comment on them.

   a. _____

   _____

   b. _____

   _____

   _____

Reading 2
FEI CEO's Top Financial Reporting Issues For 2004

Reprinted with permission from *Financial Executive*, January/February 2004.
© 2004 by Financial Executives International, 200 Campus Drive, Florham Park, NJ 07932-0674; www.fei.org.

By Ellen M. Heffes
Managing Editor

financial REPORTING — domestic NEWS

In a year of unprecedented regulation, FEI President and CEO Colleen Sayther offers the following list of 11 financial reporting issues that require the attention of financial executives during 2004. She notes they are not listed in any particular order, as the level of importance is certain to vary among companies.

1. **Internal Controls**. Ensure that you have complied with Sarbanes-Oxley Section 404, which requires management to assess its internal control environment and the external auditor to attest to the internal control environment.

2. **Variable Interest Entities (VIEs)**. Comply with FIN 46, which requires that companies consolidate variable interest entities. The rule was issued in response to Enron's off-balance-sheet treatment of such entities. It was originally supposed to take effect in the third quarter, but on October 8, FASB extended the deadline due to the significant implementation issues companies and their auditors were dealing with. There have been numerous FSPs issued related to FIN 46 attempting to address the myriad of implementation issues; review those as well (as we go to print we were at FSP #46-7). In mid-December, FASB was still looking at overhauling FIN 46 prior to the effective date of the first reporting period after Dec. 15, 2003.

3. **Pension Disclosures**. Comply with new pension disclosures. FASB is due to issue a final statement before year-end 2003 as FASB Statement No. 132 (revised 2003, rather than FASB Statement No. 51), but has tentatively decided to require additional disclosures for 2003 calendar year end companies based on comments received from its recent exposure draft.

4. **MD&A Guidance**. Comply with MD&A guidance. As we go to print, the SEC is planning to issue some additional guidance before the 2003 reporting season, which will likely suggest an "Executive Summary" section intended to highlight the important items in the MD&A. Also, ensure that your disclosures of Critical Accounting Policies are robust enough for a user to understand your business model.

5. **Revenue Recognition**. Comply with EITF 00-21, *Revenue Arrangements with Multiple Deliverables*. Also, monitor FASB's Revenue Recognition project.

6. **Off-Balance Sheet Arrangements Disclosures**. Comply with FR-67, *Disclosures of Off-Balance Sheet Arrangements and Contractual Obligations*. This was issued by the SEC in January 2003 for compliance for 2003 year-ends. This requires SEC registrants to provide an explanation of their off-balance sheet arrangements in a separately captioned subsection of the MD&A, and to provide an overview of certain known contractual obligations in a tabular format.

7. **Embrace Transparency**. Use judgment in determining items that are important for investors to better understand your company's financial position and future trends. Don't wait for rules to come out specifically requiring good disclosure.

8. **Audit Committee Governance**. Disclose your audit committee financial expert in accordance with Sarbanes-Oxley. Ensure that audit fees and non-audit-related expenses with your auditor are within independence guidelines and are appropriately approved.

9. **Financial Instruments with Characteristics of Both Liabilities and Equity**. Comply with FAS 150, *Accounting for Certain Financial Instruments with Characteristics of Both Liabilities and Equity*. This statement

requires that many financial instruments that may have previously been classified as equity, be classified as debt. It is effective in 2003, but deferred indefinitely is the effective date for certain provisions relating to certain mandatorily redeemable financial instruments.

10. **Stock Options**. Monitor FASB's project on stock options, in particular the deliberations on valuation.

11. **International Convergence**. Monitor what's going on at the International Accounting Standards Board (IASB). Whatever projects are on the IASB agenda are likely to be on FASB's agenda in the near term (including pension accounting, insurance accounting, lease accounting). In mid-December, FASB issued several Exposure Drafts identifying short-term convergence issues.

Financial Executive
January/February 2004
Page 16

Question for Consideration

Though your knowledge of accounting and financial reporting may be limited at this time, identify two or three reporting issues that you perceive as the most important. Discuss.

Name _____ Professor _____

Course _____ Section _____

Assignment 3
Initial Review of the Annual Report
and Financial Statements

Name of your company: _____

By now you should have received the Annual Report (plus SEC 10-K and proxy statement) you requested from your company. The purpose of this assignment is to review and understand the basic information that is reported in your company's Annual Report with primary emphasis on the financial statements.

Organization of the Annual Report

In general, you will find Annual Reports organized into the six different sections discussed below.

1. **Financial Highlights** – Somewhere in the first few pages or so you will find a summary of financial highlights covering as many as 10 or 20 years. Often this section contains a variety of charts and graphs. These data are not financial statements but merely a shorthand summary of the firm over a number of years.

2. **The Company and Its Products** – Near the beginning of the report, there is usually a fairly lengthy section about the company and its products. (If the company has had a good year, there will probably be lots of color pictures of the executives. If the company had a bad year, they might leave out pictures of the executives altogether.) This section of the report includes mostly public relations-type information. It's a chance for the company to brag about its products, people, and activities.

3. **Management Discussion and Analysis** – Following the public relations section of the Annual Report, you will find a section titled "Management's Discussion and Analysis." Often this section is referred to in the business press by its initials, the MD&A. Here, management is required to identify significant events, trends and developments affecting the firm and to discuss management's thinking on these matters.

4. **Financial Statements and the Notes to the Financial Statements** – Following the MD&A, you should find the financial statements and the accompanying notes. Generally, there will be a balance sheet, income statement, statement of cash flows, and a statement of stockholders' equity. Often, each financial statement will have the word "Consolidated" in its title to indicate that the corporation

owns one or more subsidiaries and that the financial results of the subsidiaries have been combined with those of the parent company to produce a single set of financial statements. The Notes are an integral part of the financial statements because they disclose the accounting methods used by the firm, provide additional detail regarding certain amounts on the face of the financial statements, and disclose additional matters not otherwise revealed by the financial statements. Financial statements without the accompanying notes comprise incomplete disclosure and can be misleading.

5. **Statement of Management Responsibility and the Report of the Independent Accountants (or Auditor's Report)** – Read them carefully. These statements reveal (1) who is responsible for the content of the financial statements and (2) whether the financial statements present fairly the financial situation of the firm.

6. **Basic Company Facts** – Following the Notes to the Financial Statements there are usually two or three pages of basic facts about the company, e.g., list of officers and directors, stock exchange listing, state of incorporation.

Completing the Assignment

1. Read the Management Discussion and Analysis (MD&A) section. What is the general tone of management's comments in this section? Was the most recent year a positive or negative experience for the company? Does management appear optimistic or pessimistic about the future? Discuss.

_____

_____

_____

_____

_____

_____

_____

_____

_____

_____

_____

_____

_____

_____

_____

2. The Income Statement

    a. What format was used to prepare your firm's income statement? (Check one)

        _____ Single-step

        _____ Multiple-step

    Hint: *If gross margin (also called gross profit) is reported on the income statement, it's the multiple-step format. Otherwise, the single-step format has been used.*

    b. Determine whether any of the following "special items" appear on the most recent income statement. They would appear near the end. Indicate below whether the item appears and (if it appears) indicate whether it increased or decreased net income. Then explain the underlying event or transaction that caused the item to arise.

	Item present?	Increase	Decrease
1) Discontinued operations	_____	_____	_____

_____

_____

_____

	Item present?	Increase	Decrease
2) Extraordinary gain (or loss)	_____	_____	_____

_____

_____

_____

	Item present?	Increase	Decrease
3) Cumulative effect of a change in accounting principle	_____	_____	_____

_____

_____

_____

    c. Using your judgment, list the *major* items of revenue and expense that are reported on your company's most recent income statement. For each item, indicate whether it is a revenue or an expense. Do not include any of the special items from Part b above.

	Revenue	Expense
1) _____	_____	_____
2) _____	_____	_____
3) _____	_____	_____
4) _____	_____	_____
5) _____	_____	_____

3. The Balance Sheet

    a. Which of the following terms describes the balance sheet as reported by your firm? (Check those that apply.)

        _____ Classified balance sheet (i.e., assets are segregated into categories)

        _____ Comparative balance sheet (i.e., more than one year of data is presented)

    b. All publicly held companies are required to prepare a three-year comparative income statement and a two-year balance sheet. Why do you think that comparative financial statements are required?

      _____

      _____

    c. If your company presented a classified balance sheet, identify the amounts your firm reported for each of the following categories and the percentage of total assets that each represents.

	Amount	Percent
1) Current assets	_____	_____
2) Property, plant, and equipment	_____	_____
3) Other long-term assets	_____	_____
4) Current liabilities	_____	_____
5) Long-term liabilities	_____	_____
6) Contributed capital	_____	_____
7) Retained earnings	_____	_____

Note

If you were a creditor of a firm (i.e., the firm owed you money) you would be interested in whether the firm had enough resources to pay you when your bill came due. Two indicators of a firm's ability to pay its bills as they become due are (1) the amount of working capital (sometimes called net working capital), and (2) the current ratio (sometimes called the working capital ratio).

Working capital (WC) is the cushion by which total current assets exceed total current liabilities.

$$WC = \text{current assets} - \text{current liabilities}$$

The current ratio (CR) reveals how many dollars of current assets are available to pay off each dollar of current liabilities.

$$CR = \frac{\text{current assets}}{\text{current liabilities}}$$

---

d. What amount of working capital did your company have as of the date of its two most recent balance sheets?

Important: If your firm didn't prepare a classified balance sheet, you can't compute the amount of working capital or the current ratio. If that's the case, skip to No. 4.

	Most Recent Balance Sheet	Next Most Recent Balance Sheet
Working capital	_____	_____

e. What was the current ratio, also known as the working capital ratio, at the end of the two most recent years? For comparison to other firms, check with five classmates (who are analyzing different firms) to see what their results were. Record those results below along with those of your firm. List the names of each comparative firm.

Alternative

As an alternative to comparing your company to those of your classmates, you may want to use four or five other companies' financial statements that you get from the Internet. These companies can be used in Assignments 4, 7, 10, 12 and 13 and can be from either your industry or different industries.

Check with your professor to make sure this alternative is acceptable.

	Most Recent Year	Next Most Recent Year
Your firm _____	_____	_____
_____	_____	_____
_____	_____	_____
_____	_____	_____
_____	_____	_____
_____	_____	_____

f. How does your firm appear to compare to the other firms you listed above regarding its ability to pay current liabilities as they become due?

_____

_____

_____

_____

_____

_____

_____

_____

4. The Statement of Cash Flows

   a. Which format does your company use to report the statement of cash flows? (check one)

   _____ Direct format   (The operating activities section begins with a Direct format line such as "Cash received from customers.")

   _____ Indirect format (The operating activities section begins with a line such as "Net income" or "Net loss" and then proceeds to add and subtract items from that amount.)

   b. In the spaces following, fill-in the proper summary amounts from your company's most recent statement of cash flows. If any of the four categories represented a net cash outflow, show that amount in parentheses.

   1) Net cash inflow (outflow) from *operating* activities   _____

   2) Net cash inflow (outflow) from *financing* activities   _____

      List the two largest transactions

      a) _____

      b) _____

   3) Net cash inflow (outflow) from *investing* activities   _____

      List the two largest transactions

      a) _____

      b) _____

   4) Net increase (decrease) in cash, or sometimes labeled net change in cash and cash equivalents, for the year   _____

   c. Now go back to the balance sheet and fill-in the following amounts that are reported for Cash (under the assets category).

   1) Current year's ending cash balance   _____

   2) Prior year's ending cash balance   _____

   3) Change in cash balance during the current year   _____

   d. Does the number on line c.3) above match the number on line b.4) above? (check one)

   1) _____ Yes   _____ No

   Hint: They should match. This is an example of financial statement articulation, which means that numbers reported on one financial statement are related to numbers on the other statements.

   2) If the amounts do not match, by how much do they differ?

   _____

5. The Statement of Stockholders' Equity

   a. Did your company include a statement of stockholders' equity with the rest of its financial statements? (check one)

      _____ Yes

      _____ No   (If no, ignore part b.)

   b. Carefully review the most recent year's data on the statement of stockholders' equity. Were there any significant changes in the amounts comprising stockholders' equity between the beginning of the year and the end of the year? If so, complete the table below for the significant changes. In the right-most column, use parentheses to indicate a balance that decreased.

      Ignore changes that you judge to be insignificant. If your company had no significant changes in the amounts comprising stockholders' equity, note that on the first line.

Statement of Stockholders' Equity Accounts	Balance at Beginning of Year	Balance at End of Year	Change in Balance During Year
_____	_____	_____	_____
_____	_____	_____	_____
_____	_____	_____	_____
_____	_____	_____	_____
_____	_____	_____	_____
_____	_____	_____	_____

6. Notes to the Financial Statements

   a. The first footnote is usually labeled something like "Summary of Significant Accounting Policies." It explains which accounting alternative that management selected to handle a particular type of transaction. Give two examples of an accounting policy disclosed in this note.

      1) _____

      2) _____

   b. What type of information is revealed in the remaining footnotes?

      _____

      _____

      _____

      _____

      _____

7. Statement of Management Responsibility and the Report of Independent Accountants

   Differentiate between the roles of a company's management and its auditor with respect to the financial statements.

   _____

   _____

   _____

   _____

   _____

   _____

   _____

8. Articulation of Financial Statements

   Articulation of Financial Statements refers to information on one financial statement being related to information on another financial statement. Find an additional example of articulation in your company's financial statements beyond the example involving cash from No. 4.d. Describe it.

   _____

   _____

   _____

   _____

   _____

   _____

   _____

   _____

Reading 3
Watch Your Mouth

Reprinted from the December 2003 issue of *CFO*. © 2003 CFO Publishing Corp.
For more information about reprints from *CFO*, contact PARS International Corp. at 212-221-9595.

By Lori Calabro
Deputy Editor

As Reg FD enters its fourth year, enforcements so far offer hints on how to communicate.

When regulation fair disclosure took effect in October 2000, finance executives felt some trepidation that their own words might eventually hang them. As a company's main spokesperson on matters financial, after all, a CFO is in the precarious position of routinely answering analysts' and shareholders' questions—especially about earnings prospects.

The initial wariness has eased a bit. Reg FD's effort to standardize the flow of corporate information to all interested parties has resulted in only five completed federal investigations of violations so far. Four became public in November 2002, and the latest, involving pharmaceuticals giant Schering-Plough Corp., emerged this past September (see "Recapping a Reg," at the end of this article). [*Table not included.*] There's also been just one high-profile CFO casualty: Raytheon Co.'s Franklyn Caine resigned in December 2002, a few weeks after the Securities and Exchange Commission named him in a selective-disclosure action.

But the SEC is still watching. "We've got a number of active investigations in the pipeline," SEC enforcement director Stephen Cutler recently told a group of lawyers at Georgetown University. And Boris Feldman, a securities lawyer with Wilson Sonsini Goodrich & Rosati in Palo Alto, California, says the SEC's regional bureaus are busy "reviewing Reg FD violations" and questioning CFOs about unexplained stock movements.

"We've got a number of active investigations in the pipeline," says Stephen Cutler, the SEC' enforcement director.

Still, the enforcement actions taken to date—which Gordon McCoun, senior managing director of New York based investor-relations firm Financial Dynamics, says target the "most visible and the most obvious transgressions"—are instructive. Feldman, in fact, finds them "quite interesting from an anthropological perspective," and likens the SEC to Talmudic scholars who "have set markers out there." And in response, companies continue to reshape their communication strategies, says McCoun.

In fact, says Robert Profusek, a partner at the New York office of law firm Jones Day, taken together, the SEC's actions have put companies on notice that they can no longer make selective disclosure errors—a conclusion especially obvious after the recent sanction against Schering-Plough. "It's very clear that the incidents [investigated] so far were mistakes, not intentional bad behavior," he explains. But under today's more mature Reg FD, he says, the SEC has zero tolerance for any "accidental" missteps.

Between the Lines There's no question that companies are now taking a more uniform approach to dealing with the external flow of material information. "Reg FD codified what would be fair and balanced disclosure," says R. Kevin Matz, a senior vice president at $4.5 billion Emcor Group Inc., and a spokesman for the Norwalk, Connecticut, company. Moreover, the rule "has achieved its main objective—it has leveled the playing field," says Chuck Hill, director of research at First Call. "It's forcing analysts to get back to the basics of analysis."

For companies, the new procedures are now almost habit, says Matz. An April survey by the National Investor Relations Institute found that of the 92 percent of companies that conduct earnings conference calls, all use Webcasts or teleconferencing. And in June, NIRI found that one-on-ones and small group meetings with analysts and investors seem to be as popular as ever—an indication that companies are comfortable staying within the confines of the rule.

That doesn't mean everyone is happy with the information being provided. Indeed, Wall Street, which vigorously opposed Reg FD, continues to fume. The Securities Industry Association, its trade group, declares that "the regulation has had the impact the association feared: less information, lower quality, higher costs, and greater volatility."

And Wall Street is particularly upset with the parade of companies that have stopped giving guidance. The trend really started last December, when the Atlanta-based Coca-Cola Co. vowed not to provide quarterly or annual guidance, and companies like McDonald's and AT&T followed suit. They may not be the last. The April NIRI survey found that, overall, 28 percent of companies are considering eliminating guidance.

Material Breaches The stated idea behind restricting guidance, of course, is to refocus analysts on long term rather than quarterly results. But CFOs know that it also means material slips are less likely to occur. Material revelations have been at the root of the actionable cases to date. So, it's little wonder that in a poll of finance executives two years ago, Pricewaterhouse-Coopers found that 68 percent wanted the SEC to issue specific guidelines about which information is material and requires disclosure, and which is not.

Some slipups under Reg FD represent seemingly obvious breaches, however. In one case,

against Siebel Systems Inc., CEO Thomas Siebel allegedly disclosed material information at an invitation-only technology conference, assuming that it would be Webcast. Last November, Siebel became the first company to pay a fine—of $250,000—to settle a Reg FD case. It promised not to selectively disclose again, but the real message—one CFOs should take to heart, says Feldman—is that Siebel "wouldn't have gotten into trouble if it had Webcast." (As CFO went to press, Siebel revealed in its third-quarter financials that the SEC was investigating it for a second Reg FD violation. The potential enforcement action reportedly involves statements made by CFO Ken Goldman at an April 30 dinner with analysts.)

The Schering-Plough case should worry CFOs, because it's no longer "what you say, but how you say it."

The message in the Raytheon case is that material breaches can also get personal. Former CFO Caine didn't give quarterly guidance during an initial conference call in February 2001. Then, shortly thereafter, he allegedly made calls to individual analysts, telling them their estimates were too high. According to the SEC's enforcement action, the problem leading to the sanction was Caine's knowledge that "Raytheon had provided no public quarterly earnings guidance for 2001" when he made those calls.

Even when the SEC only issues a report instead of taking enforcement action, there are lessons. In the case of Motorola

Inc., the company said during a conference call that it was experiencing "significant weakness" in sales. The IR officer later allegedly told some analysts the decline in sales would be about 25 percent, after the general counsel advised him that the number was not material. The SEC's decision against taking an enforcement action reflected its finding that the advice, while unsound, was given in good faith. The take-away? "When in doubt, check with a lawyer," says Feldman, with a chuckle.

Experts' views on possible lessons from the latest Reg FD case are mixed. Feldman believes the Schering-Plough case "dwarfs the prior enforcements" and "may signal a policy shift, because it now is not just what you say, but how you say it." At issue is one line in the September enforcement action against the $10 billion company and former CEO Richard Kogan. There, the SEC noted that Schering-Plough violated Reg FD "through a combination of spoken language, tone, emphasis, and demeanor" —a phrase that has sent some lawyers searching for duct tape.

Still, if you read the complaint, says Louis Thompson Jr., NIRI's CEO, "what Kogan said was more than adequate" to constitute a material breach of Reg FD. In fact, during the 2002 meetings cited—an initial closed-door meeting with three big shareholders and a follow-up meeting with analysts and investors—Kogan allegedly said that the company's 2003 earnings would be "terrible," among other things. That led the stock to fall more than 17 percent. (Troubles at Schering-Plough also led to the departure of CFO Jack Wyszomierski in November.)

But it was the SEC's reaction to the downbeat way the remarks were delivered that has given companies and general counsels the most pause. "Body language is a tough legal standard," says Stuart Kaswell, a partner with Dechert LLP in Washington, D.C. To be on the safe side, says Feldman, CFOs and CEOs should guard against looking "depressed when they talk to analysts." And since that may be impossible to do, Feldman advises companies to reevaluate the form in which they choose to communicate to Wall Street. The ruling "could be the death knell for one-on-ones," he says.

Clamming Up Such advice is leading to something of a standoff between lawyers and IR professionals. "There's a natural tug-of-war between communications and legal anyway," says McCoun. The Schering-Plough case, however, has led to "a tendency to retreat and say we are not going to give one-on-ones," he says.

At Emcor, Matz says that smaller meetings are necessary, and that the company has done a good job of self-policing its comments there. For one thing, Matz limits the number of communicators as a way of guarding against Reg FD violations. "I don't think FD is out there to trick people," he says. But by limiting Emcor's spokesmen to CEO Frank MacInnis and himself, the former treasurer says, the company doesn't "deviate from protocol" and "keeps the information standard."

Limiting the time spent communicating is another way companies avoid accidental transgressions. "But the best brightline rule is to have a permanent quiet period except for one day per quarter," says Feldman. That is when a company releases earnings. Then, it should "give guidance with enough variables for analysts to draw conclusions"—and say no more. He calls this the only "viable and secure approach for a CFO."

Other safeguards continue to evolve. While most companies Webcast their own earnings announcements, for example, many now insist that outside investor-conference sponsors offer the Webcast. In fact, the June NIRI survey found that 21 percent of companies refuse to participate in such events unless they are Webcast in that manner. That approach, says Feldman, should extend to the breakout sessions at those conferences, which he terms the "Wild West" of investor relations.

The main guideline from the Reg FD violations: "If business will not meet expectations, don't do [any] meetings," says McCoun. "Or if you still do the meeting, don't do it until you put out a new set of expectations." Reg FD is not meant to clamp down on information, he says. Instead, it formalizes "what the best communication practices are."

Those policies are still subject to SEC scrutiny, however. And as far as enforcement is concerned, Feldman says, "the end point of the journey is not clear yet. We're just on the bleeding edge."

CFO
December 2003
Pages 73 - 75

Questions for Consideration

1. Do you believe that the SEC has gone too far in its interpretation of Reg FD? Explain.

2. Discuss the impact on the major players affected by Reg FD, i.e., the SEC, users (both investors and analysts), and both the company's spokesperson and lawyer.

Assignment 4
The SEC 10-K Report and Proxy Statement

The Securities and Exchange Commission (SEC), an agency of the federal government, was established by the Securities Exchange Act of 1934 to promote full-disclosure of all material financial facts and other information concerning securities offered for public sale. The SEC's primary mission is to protect investors and maintain the integrity of the securities markets. Nothing can prevent the purchase of risky or low-quality securities, but the SEC strives to make sure that investors are fully informed as to the nature of their investment.

The purpose of this assignment is for you to understand the similarities and differences between a company's Annual Report to Shareholders and its SEC Form 10-K which must be submitted to the SEC annually. In addition, you will review your firm's proxy statement and evaluate certain information from it.

Name of your company: _____

In general, companies having assets of $10 million or more and 500 or more stockholders are subject to SEC regulation if their securities (e.g., stocks or bonds) are traded publicly. Principal among those regulations is the filing of regular public reports with the Commission. While there are more than a dozen different reporting forms used by SEC registrants, the three most commonly used reporting documents are the following SEC forms.

- 10-Q – the quarterly report to the SEC

- 8-K – an as-needed report of unscheduled events or corporate changes important to shareholders or the SEC. For example, when a company changes independent auditors it must announce that event by filing an 8-K with the SEC.

- 10-K – the annual report to the SEC

The 10-K is, by far, the best known of the SEC-required reports. In essence, it is a special version of the company's Annual Report. In this assignment you will learn how these are similar and how these are different. You will also discover that interesting information is disclosed in the proxy statement.

(The assignment continues on the next page.)

On the Internet

Since 1996 the SEC has required all public companies to make their required SEC filings (e.g., 10-Qs, 8-Ks, 10-Ks) electronically. These filings are then posted to the SEC's web site within 24 hours. This system is called EDGAR, which stands for Electronic Data Gathering, Analysis, and Retrieval.

You can access EDGAR by going to the Hock homepage at **hock.swlearning.com**, selecting "assignments," and looking under Assignment 4.

Completing the Assignment

The outline of this assignment is as follows. First, you are to identify each of the required sections of the SEC 10-K and indicate where they appear in your company's 10-K report. Second, you are asked to assess the similarities and differences between the information contained in your company's SEC 10-K and its Annual Report. Third, you are asked to record certain specific information about your company that is disclosed on the proxy statement.

1. The SEC 10-K Report is comprised of 14 items organized into four parts as shown below. Review your company's SEC Form 10-K and note the page(s) where each item is reported.

	Page(s) Where Item Is Reported
Part I	
Item 1. Business	_____
Item 2. Properties	_____
Item 3. Legal Proceedings	_____
Item 4. Submission of Matters to Vote of Security Holders	_____
Part II	
Item 5. Market for the Registrant's Common Equity and Related Stockholder Matters	_____
Item 6. Selected Financial Data	_____
Item 7. Management's Discussion and Analysis of Financial Condition and Results of Operations	_____
Item 8. Financial Statements and Supplementary Data	_____
Item 9. Changes in and Disagreements with Accountants on Accounting and Financial Disclosure	_____

Part III

Item 10. Directors and Executive Officers of the Registrant _____

Item 11. Executive Compensation _____

Item 12. Security Ownership of Certain Beneficial
Owners and Management _____

Item 13. Certain Relationships and Related Transactions _____

Part IV

Item 14. Exhibits, Financial Statement Schedules,
and Reports on Form 8-K _____

2. After carefully comparing your firm's annual report to its SEC 10-K, answer the following questions.

a. What information did you find in both the annual report and the SEC 10-K?

_____

_____

_____

_____

_____

_____

_____

_____

_____

b. What information is found in one document that is not found in the other?

_____

_____

_____

_____

_____

_____

_____

_____

_____

_____

_____

c. Why do you think these differences exist?

_____

_____

_____

_____

_____

_____

_____

_____

3. Answer the following questions based on information disclosed in the proxy statement.

a. Identify the date and location of the stockholders' meeting announced in the proxy statement.

Date _____

Location _____

b. Briefly describe the proposals, issues, or topics that were scheduled for action at the stockholders' meeting.

_____

_____

_____

_____

_____

c. For your firm's highest paid executive, compute the total dollar amount of compensation (e.g., salary + bonus + etc.) that he/she received from the company in each of the last three years.

For perspective about how your firm's highest paid executive compares to those of other firms, check with five classmates (who are studying different firms than you) and record their information below also. To conserve space, record information in thousands of dollars (000's).

Alternative

As an alternative to comparing your company's highest paid executive to those of your classmates' companies, you may want to compare with the companies you used in No. 3.e. of Assignment 3.

Check with your professor to make sure this option is acceptable.

Highest Paid Executive's Total Compensation	Your Firm	COMPARATIVE FIRMS				
		Firm 1	Firm 2	Firm 3	Firm 4	Firm 5
Most recent year	_____	_____	_____	_____	_____	_____
Next most recent year	_____	_____	_____	_____	_____	_____
Next most recent year	_____	_____	_____	_____	_____	_____

d. How does the total compensation of your firm's highest-paid executive compare to the highest-paid executives of your comparative firms over the past three years? Discuss.

_____

_____

_____

_____

_____

_____

_____

_____

_____

_____

e. Inspect the stock performance graph near the end of the proxy statement. How does the price performance of the company's stock compare to that of other companies? Does the trend in stock returns match the trend in compensation being earned by the company's top executives? Discuss.

_____

_____

_____

_____

_____

_____

_____

_____

_____

_____

4. Optional Memo No. 1 – Company Background

Having completed the first four assignments of the **FRP**, you have acquired sufficient information about your company and its industry to prepare the first memo to your client. Though there are four separate memos, together they will develop an overall assessment of your company.

For format see page -iv- in the Preface or follow your professor's instructions.

Guide for Memo No. 1

a. State your *initial reaction* about your company , i.e., favorable or unfavorable.

In your analysis you may want to consider the following:

- ▸ your company's industry;

- ▸ its major products or services;

- ▸ general economic and political environment; and

- ▸ your company's position in the industry, i.e., does it appear to be a leader (pro-active) or follower (reactionary)?

b. Does your company's overall disclosure system—its annual report and SEC filings (10-K and proxy)—appear to contain sufficient information to allow you to gain a working knowledge about your company? Explain.

Reading 4
Unlocking the Secrets of a Proxy Statement

Reprinted from the March 4, 2002, issue of *Business Week* by permission. © 2002 by The McGraw-Hill Companies.

By Susan Scherreik

The Fine Print
These dense documents deserve close inspection.

The corporate proxy statement—which most public companies will issue over the next three months—is fast becoming required reading. Now that Enron's implosion has raised concerns that cronyism and poor corporate governance might be commonplace, investors should pay closer attention to these dense legal documents, which provide details about the pay and perks of a company's top executives, directors, and outside accountants. "You need to determine whether you can rely on the directors and top management to act responsibly when things go bad," says Ken Bertsch, director of corporate governance at TIAA-CREF, which manages $290 billion in assets. "The proxy statement can help you do that."

Tyco International, for one, has firsthand experience of the closer scrutiny investors are giving proxies. The day after it filed its latest statement with the Securities & Exchange Commission on Jan. 28, investors pushed Tyco's share price down 20%. The reason? A disclosure that Tyco paid $10 million to an outside director and another $10 million to a charity he controlled fanned concerns about potential conflicts of interest. The company said the payments were for the director's help in arranging an acquisition. This came on top of worries about accounting irregularities that already had pummeled Tyco shares.

Companies typically file proxy statements about six weeks before their annual meeting to inform investors when and where the session will be held. If you're a shareholder, you'll get the statement in the mail. Or you can obtain any public company's proxy statement via the SEC's EDGAR database (www.edgar-online.com). The statements are listed on EDGAR as form DEF 14A filings.

What should you look for in a proxy statement? Start with the "Summary Compensation Table." Here, you'll see how much the CEO and the four highest-paid executives earned annually over the past three fiscal years in salary, bonus, stock options, and any other compensation. If the execs got raises, check if the hikes are in line with those at similar companies. To help you wade through the legalese, the AFL-CIO's Web site defines common proxy statement terms at www.aflcio.org. Click on Executive PayWatch, then database, then proxy statement.

As for bonuses, this year you probably won't see the big numbers of the 1990s. But be on the lookout for signs that companies are making up for skimpy bonuses by handing out overly generous stock option grants, says Bertsch. At Cisco, for instance, CEO John Chambers and the four highest-paid executives received zip in bonuses in fiscal 2001 that ended July 31 (table). [Not reproduced here.] Although Cisco lost $1 billion in the year, Chambers received option grants worth an estimated $121.6 million, while four senior vice-presidents each got at least $13 million in grants. Cisco spokeswoman Terry Anderson says the grants' size is based on industry standards. Shareholders benefit, she adds, because employee stock options encourage long- term commitment.

For more detail on stock options, flip to a table called "Options Grants in the Last Fiscal Year." Here, companies estimate what the options grants would be worth based either on the Black-Scholes options pricing model, or the assumption that the company's stock rises 5% and 10% annually over the options' life.

The options grants section will also tell you whether a company has repriced previously granted options for top execs. When a stock's market price falls far below the option purchase price—a common occurrence over the past two years—some companies cancel the old options and substitute new ones that will turn profitable at a lower price. This can be a cause for concern because it signals to execs they'll be rewarded no matter what. The Investor Responsibility Research Center, which analyzes proxy statements for institutional investors, found that in the past year or so, 111 of the approximately 2,000 companies it reviews, including Sprint and Novell, repriced options for some top executives.

Also scan the employee compensation section for unusual gifts or payments. Mattel's 2000 proxy statement disclosed that departing CEO Jill Barad's contract gave her $7.2 million in loan forgiveness and $3.3 million to cover personal tax expenses.

Are company directors cronies of the CEO or an independent group acting on behalf of shareholders? To find out, look at the directors' brief biographies listed in the "Election of Directors" section. The majority of directors shouldn't be company employees, and they ideally should have experience managing similar companies.

Other must-reads are "Related Party Transactions" and "Certain Relationships." Is an outside director's son employed at the firm? You'll find out here. More important, these sections will tell you whether directors are moonlighting for the company in ways that could conflict with their role as management watchdog. "You want to see that outside directors are really independent, not the investment bankers, lawyers, or outside vendors of the firm," says Howard Schilit, director of the Center for Financial Research & Analysis. For example, Costco's latest proxy statement reveals that it paid one outside director's company $1.5 million for providing insurance, while a second director's company got $1.3 million for merchandise sold to the discount retailer. Costco CEO James Sinegal said doing business with outside directors is not necessarily a conflict of interest. In these instances Costco asked for competitive bids – and those directors' companies had the best prices, he said.

Check the "Director Compensation" section for data on directors' stock holdings. Outside directors should own a good chunk of company stock to align their interests with shareholders. That's why you need to check the footnotes to see how much of the total stock holdings are in options grants. One rule of thumb: Longtime directors should have company stock holdings equal to three years of their annual retainer.

The section on accountants is also important reading. Last year, the SEC for the first time required companies to reveal the additional fees they pay auditors – and the disclosures have proved interesting. Enron's auditor, Arthur Andersen, was criticized for multimillion-dollar contracts, which exceeded the auditing fees it earned. At Agilent Technologies, for fiscal 2001 ended Oct. 31, auditor compensation included $15.2 million for various services, on top of audit fees of $2.9 million.

Investors learned from Enron that it's important to get a sense of how the company treats its insiders. The proxy statement is an essential guide through that culture.

Business Week
March 4, 2002
Pages 108 - 109

Questions for Consideration

1. The proxy statement normally is a separate *booklet* that accompanies the annual report to shareholders. It usually is not printed on glossy paper with colored pictures. Would its appearance discourage investors from reading it? Explain.

2. Which of the five basic sections of the proxy statement do you think is the most important? Discuss.

Name _____   Professor _____

Course _____   Section _____

Assignment 5
The Accounting Profession

The purpose of this assignment is to learn about the independent accounting firm that audited your company's financial statements. You will also have an opportunity to further develop your library research skills. (Make no mistake about it, these skills are valued by employers. They expect you to know how to find business information about potential customers, suppliers, competitors, or firms that might be potential acquisitions.)

Key References for this Assignment

Category 1 Sources

1. *Hoover's Handbook of Private Companies 2004*, Hoover's, Inc.

2. *D & B Million Dollar Directory*, Dun & Bradstreet

Category 2 Sources

1. *ABI Inform*, UMI Inc. (online only)

2. *Business NewsBank*, NewsBank, Inc.

3. *Business Periodicals Index*, H.W. Wilson Company

4. *Business Source Premier*, (via Ebsco Host)

5. *F&S Index United States*, Predicasts

6. *The New York Times Index*, New York Times Company

7. *The Wall Street Journal Index*, Dow Jones & Company

Completing the Assignment

1. Name of your company _____

2. Name of your company's auditor _____

3. Size of the accounting firm

    The purpose of this section is to demonstrate that the public accounting firms that audit large U.S. companies are, generally, very large companies themselves. The "Big Four" accounting firms (Deloitte and Touche; Ernst and Young; KPMG; and PricewaterhouseCoopers) all had revenues in 2003 between

$12 and $15 billion dollars. Odds are that your firm was audited by one of these companies.

Use either of the Key References in Category 1 to determine the following information about your firm's independent auditor. If your library does not have either of these references, the Reference Librarian probably can suggest alternative sources from which to obtain the data.

On the Internet

The information needed for this assignment is usually included at the accounting firm's website, although you may have to hunt for it.

You can access your auditor's website by going to the Hock homepage at **hock.swlearning.com.** Select "assignments" and then Assignment 5.

---

a. Where is the home office of your company's auditor?

    _____

b. How many employees does the accounting firm have? _____

c. Indicate whether this is the number of U.S. employees, employees worldwide, or whether this cannot be determined.

    _____

    The year for which this information pertains _____

d. What is the annual revenue of the accounting firm that audited your corporation?

    _____

    The year for which this information pertains _____

e. What services does your accounting firm offer besides auditing (now referred to as "assurance")?

    _____

    _____

    _____

    _____

    _____

    _____

    _____

    _____

    _____

4. Current issues facing your company's independent auditor

   Use one or more of the Key References in Category 2 (or the Internet) to identify recent articles about your company's independent auditor. Generally, focus on articles that are no more than two years old. Select two recent articles concerning your firm's auditor (no more than one article from a single index). Find articles that you believe convey significant and interesting information. Photocopy them to turn in with this assignment.

   a. Index used to find article #1 _____

   b. Citation for article #1

      1) Name of periodical _____

      2) Date of article _____

      3) Title of article _____

      4) Page numbers _____

   c. Article analysis

      Why is this article significant and interesting? Use complete sentences and limit your response to no more than 100 words.

      _____
      _____
      _____
      _____
      _____
      _____
      _____
      _____
      _____
      _____
      _____
      _____
      _____
      _____
      _____
      _____
      _____
      _____

    d. Index used to find article #2 _____

    e. Citation for article #2

        1) Name of periodical _____

        2) Date of article _____

        3) Title of article _____

        4) Page numbers _____

    f. Article analysis

    Why is this article significant and interesting? Use complete sentences and limit your response to no more than 100 words.

_____

_____

_____

_____

_____

_____

_____

_____

_____

_____

_____

_____

_____

_____

_____

_____

5. Attach photocopies of the articles to this assignment.

    Note: It is a serious breach of academic integrity to tear articles out of magazines that do not belong to you, e.g., those in the library. Please don't do it!

Reading 5
Introduction to Forensic Accounting

Reprinted from *National Public Accountant*, the journal of the National Society of Accountants, June 2003.

By Frank J Grippo, MBA, CPA
Associate Professor of Accounting and Law, William Patterson University
and
J.W. "Ted" Ibex, MBA, CPA, ABV
Partner in Rosenfarb Winters, LLC, Tinton Falls, NJ

Forensic accounting is a science (i.e., a department of systemized knowledge) that deals with the application of accounting facts gathered through auditing methods and procedures to legal problems usually dealing with financial and valuation issues. It is very different from traditional auditing. Forensic accounting is the investigation of an allegation; the evidence is expected to be presented in a judicial forum. Forensic accountants often employ specialists in other areas as part of a team to gather evidence. There must be absolute assurance before evidence is presented in court.

The scope of the investigation may be limited to specific issues. The financial wherewithal of the client is a key factor in determining the depth of a forensic investigation. Forensic services may be very costly. It is important for the client to understand, from the onset, the costs to finance the litigation. There should be a cost/benefit relationship. There are a few principled people who will want to spend a dollar to recover 50 cents, but they are not the norm.

Forensic accounting inte-grates investigative, accounting and auditing skills. Forensic accountants look at documents in a critical manner in order to draw conclusions and to calculate values. They review financial and other data to identify irregular patterns and/or suspicious transactions—always with an awareness of areas ripe for fraud. Forensic accountants don't merely look at the numbers—they look behind the numbers.

The marked increases in white-collar crime and business disputes and other claims have helped created the need for forensic accounting. It is used in a variety of situations including but not limited to, the following

- Business valuations
- Divorce proceedings and matrimonial disputes
- Personal injury and fatal accident claims
- Professional negligence
- Insurance claims evaluations
- Arbitration
- Partnership and corporation disputes
- Shareholder disputes (minority shareholders claiming oppression)
- Civil and criminal actions concerning fraud and financial irregularities
- Fraud and white-collar crime investigations.

AREAS OF FORENSIC ACCOUNTING

Forensic accounting can be divided into two areas of specialization—litigation support and investigation or fraud accounting. Litigation support specialists concern themselves with business valuation, economic damages, testimony as expert witnesses future earnings evaluation and income and expense analysis. Fraud accountants apply their skills to investigate areas of alleged criminal misconduct in order to support or dispel damages. Because these fields overlap, a forensic accountant may do litigation support work one month and perhaps act as a fraud accountant on another engagement the following month. More likely, the forensic accountant will be working on several types of engagements simultaneously.

Litigation Support

This is a situation where the forensic accountant is asked to give an opinion on either facts that are known or those that have yet to be uncovered. The forensic accountant is an integral part of the legal team. In this capacity, he/-she helps to substantiate allegations, analyze facts, dispute claims, and develop motives. The amount of involvement and point at which the forensic accountant gets involved varies from case to case. Sometimes the forensic accountant is called upon from the beginning of the case; at other times the forensic accountant is only retained before the case is scheduled to go to court and after out-of-court settlements have failed.

In litigation support, the forensic accountant assists in obtaining documentation to support or dispel a claim. He/she may be called upon to review documentation in order to give an assessment of the case to the legal team and/or identify areas where a loss occurred. Moreover, the forensic accountant may be asked to get involved during the discovery stage to help formulate questions. He/she may also be asked to review the report of the opposing expert witness and give an evaluation of its strengths and weaknesses. During trial the forensic accountant may serve as an expert witness, help to provide questions for cross examination, and assist with settlement discussions.

Investigations

Investigations often involve fraud and are associated with criminal matters. Typically an investigative accounting assignment would result from a client's suspicion that there is employee fraud. Employees are responsible for about 75 percent of all fraud; approximately 55 percent of all fraud is discovered as a result of strong internal controls.

Fraud is a permanent risk in any and all businesses. Regulatory agencies, police forces and attorneys may retain a forensic accountant to investigate securities fraud, kickbacks, insurance fraud, money-laundering schemes, and asset search and analysis.

BUSINESS VALUATION ISSUES

Business valuation is a discipline unto itself. The forensic accountant needs additional education in business appraisal theory and science beyond typical accounting training. Because business appraisal is a specialized discipline, a separate designation, Accredited Business Valuation (ABV), is awarded after passing a comprehensive examination. To maintain the ABV designation, continuing education is required.

The well-informed forensic accountant can provide invaluable service with regard to business appraisal and the numerous issues that can and do arise. The existence of buy-sell agreements and purchase offers from third parties, for example, can impact the appraisal process and evaluation. For the forensic accountant of today, the education process does not stop. Business valuation is an evolving science. You must constantly be on the alert for new developments to continue to be an effective provider of service to the legal community.

It is worth mentioning that the forensic investigation is important to establish what the true income of the business is. What you see in the published income statement may not paint the real picture of the earnings of the business.

Nothing from college training, experience in public accounting, or employment in private industry can completely prepare a forensic accountant for the variety of emotional levels displayed in litigious situations, especially when substantial sums of money are involved. Even

though some things may appear trivial, they are not to the litigants. When you are on the "wrong" side of a case, whatever you say about the value of a business or the extent of the impact of questionable activities is going to be suspect. Of course, if you come up with the wrong "answers" for your client, he/she may be upset with you as well.

It is very important that a forensic accountant be able to deal with people involved in emotionally charged situations. Only experience brings that ability. Experience linked with strong communication skills goes a long way in being able to be effective with a variety of people and their attitudes.

SKILLS

What skills do forensic accountants need to provide litigation support to attorneys and to conduct investigations to assist their clients?

One of the most important skills is experience in a career gained from working day to day. We all have acquired skills in accounting and auditing, taxation, business operations and management, internal controls, interpersonal relationships, communication, and, without claiming backgrounds in psychology, people. It is a matter of maturing in the profession. Knowledge of how businesses operate and of effective systems of internal controls and procedures are critical. Knowledge must be both technical and practical.

The education process never ends. The expert who knows everything is dangerous. A closed mind will ultimately spell disaster to all involved.

The training one gets in dealing with people who no longer like each other is invaluable. The forensic accountant is going to make someone unhappy. That person could be your own client. But a forensic accountant still must be able to get information from "friend" and "foe" alike. Granted, you may get help from the attorney and the court. However, any experienced forensic accountant becomes somewhat of an expert in dealing with diverse and opposing personalities. This takes skill and lots of time. Emotions often run high.

At the end of the day, communicating results in an understandable form to the client and attorney is the most important ingredient for success. Communications take many forms: written report, oral report, telephone conversations with various parties, giving testimony at deposition and trial, conference calls with the court, settlement conferences and so on. If you cannot communicate, your knowledge and skills and their application become almost meaningless.

In summary, effective forensic accounting requires:
- Education and training.
- Advanced and continued education in appropriate disciplines, such as business appraisal.
- Diversified accounting and auditing experience—public and private.
- Communication skills—oral and written.
- Practical business experience.
- Diversified forensic auditing experience.
- Ability to work in team environment.
- People skills and flexibility.

Finally, most important to a forensic accountant is his/her reputation and the attributes of independence and objectivity. Excellent credibility, professional standards, and ethics are essential. Being able to "think straight, talk straight" is a highly desirable attribute for a forensic accountant. Your next job depends on your last performance and your reputation.

National Public Accountant
June 2003
Pages 4 - 5

Questions for Consideration

1. Briefly discuss the difference between litigation support and fraud accounting.

2. What primary skills and attributes are identified as being necessary for a forensic accountant?

Assignment 6
The Income Statement

Name of your company _____

The purpose of this assignment is to obtain an in-depth understanding of your company's income statement as shown in the annual report and SEC 10-K. Information will be reviewed regarding revenues, expenses, income taxes, "special items," and subsequent events. In addition, you will conduct a basic financial analysis of the income statement.

Completing the assignment

1. Summarize the basic information on your company's income statements for the most recent three years. If an item was not reported, indicate by placing NA (for not applicable) in the space provided.

Basic Income Statement Information	Most Recent Year	Next Most Recent Year	Second Most Recent Year
a. Sales (total revenues)	_____	_____	_____
b. Cost of goods sold (CGS)	_____	_____	_____
c. Gross margin, profit or income	_____	_____	_____
d. Total other revenues, expenses, gains and losses (other than CGS)	_____	_____	_____
e. Income (loss) before taxes	_____	_____	_____
f. Income taxes	_____	_____	_____
g. Net income (loss)	_____	_____	_____
h. Comprehensive income	_____	_____	_____

This might be reported on a separate schedule rather than on the face of the income statement.

2. "Special items" are not typical and do not appear on all income statements. Identify any special items that appear on your company's income statements:

    ▸ income (or loss) from discontinued operations,

    ▸ extraordinary gain (or loss), and

    ▸ cumulative effect of a change in accounting principle.

If any of these special items appeared on any of the income statements for the last three years, check the item, indicate the year and the amount, and explain the underlying event/transaction that caused the item to arise.

Hint*: These events usually are explained in the Notes to the Financial Statements.*

a. _____ Income (or loss) from discontinued operations

        Year _____   Amount _____

_____

_____

_____

_____

_____

_____

_____

b. _____ Extraordinary gain (or loss)

        Year _____   Amount _____

_____

_____

_____

_____

_____

_____

_____

c. _____ Cumulative effect of a change in accounting principle

        Year _____   Amount _____

_____

_____

_____

_____

_____

_____

_____

Note

Earnings per share (EPS) is one of the most commonly used measures of a company's profitability. In its simplest form, EPS is calculated by dividing net income by the number of common shares outstanding. Though an intuitive concept, the computation can become quite complex.

Two EPS figures—*basic* and *diluted*—are required to be disclosed on the income statement. They differ essentially in the number of shares considered outstanding.

▸ Basic EPS uses only those shares actually outstanding during the period.

▸ Diluted EPS uses shares outstanding as well as shares that could become outstanding under certain circumstances, e.g., stock options are exercised.

---

3. Find your company's Net Income EPS for the current year.

    a. Indicate each EPS and the number of shares used to calculate them.

        1) Basic EPS _____ ; Number of shares _____

        2) Diluted EPS _____ ; Number of shares _____

    b. If your basic and diluted EPS figures differ, by how much do they differ?

        _____ What reason(s) can you give for this difference?

        Hint: Reasons for the difference are normally found in the EPS footnote.

        _____

        _____

        _____

        _____

        _____

        _____

4. In the Notes to the Financial Statements there should be a section with a title such as "Income Taxes." Read that carefully before completing the following section.

    a. What is the federal tax rate on corporations? _____
       (often called the *statutory tax rate*)

    b. What *effective tax rate* (sometimes called the *actual tax rate*) did your firm pay? _____

c. If the firm's *effective* or *actual tax rate* was different from the *federal* or *statutory rate,* list up to three items that caused them to differ.

_____

_____

_____

d. What was the firm's total income tax expense (in dollars) for the most recent year? _____

Note

Deferred taxes can be tax liabilities or tax assets.

▸ *Deferred tax liabilities* will be paid on profits which the company has reported on its income statement but that don't need to be paid to the government until some future date.

▸ *Deferred tax assets* represent taxes that have been paid ahead of time.

---

e. Check which type(s) of deferred taxes your company had.

_____ Deferred tax assets

_____ Deferred tax liabilities

f. Did your company have short-term and/or long-term deferred tax assets/ liabilities?

_____ Short-term

_____ Long-term

If your company had both, which is more significant? _____

g. Did the amount of your company's most significant deferred tax asset/ liability increase or decrease during the most recent year?

_____

h. By what amount did deferred taxes change from the prior year?

_____

i. List up to three examples of temporary differences that caused your firm to report deferred taxes.

_____

_____

_____

> ## Note
> A *subsequent event* is a significant event or transaction that occurs after the balance sheet date but before the annual report is distributed, e.g., the obtaining of a large contract or an unfavorable result from a major lawsuit. Failure to disclose this type of event could render the financial statements misleading.

5. Did your firm disclose any subsequent events? If so, briefly describe them.

   Hint: They usually are reported in one of the last notes to the financial statements.

   _____

   _____

   _____

   _____

   _____

   _____

   _____

   _____

   _____

   _____

> ## Note
> To determine a company's profitability trends, a percentage analysis of successive years' income statements is often prepared. This analysis frequently is referred to as preparation of *common-size income statements*. In addition, profit margins usually are computed and compared to the profit margin data of other firms.
>
> On a common-size income statement, each item is expressed as a percentage of net sales revenue. Sales revenue is arbitrarily set to equal 100% and everything else is related to it. For example, if cost of goods sold were $300 and sales were $400, cost of goods sold would be listed on the common-size income statement as 75% ($300/$400).
>
> Every item on the income statement is divided by sales. This type of statement will reveal specific trends in revenue and expense items across the years that otherwise would be obscured by growing (or decreasing) sales.

6. Prepare a percentage analysis (common-size income statements) for the most recent three years. Special items, such as discontinued operations, extraordinary items, and cumulative effects are not included in the analysis because they are not expected to recur.

   a. Complete the table below

Income Statement Item	Most Recent Year (% of Sales)	Next Most Recent Year (% of Sales)	Second Most Recent Year (% of Sales)
Sales revenue	100%	100%	100%
Cost of goods sold	_____	_____	_____
Gross margin	_____	_____	_____
Operating expenses	_____	_____	_____
_____	_____	_____	_____
_____	_____	_____	_____
_____	_____	_____	_____
_____	_____	_____	_____
Total operating expenses	_____	_____	_____
Operating income	_____	_____	_____
Other (non-operating) revenues, expenses, gains and losses			
_____	_____	_____	_____
_____	_____	_____	_____
_____	_____	_____	_____
Income before taxes	_____	_____	_____
Provision for income taxes	_____	_____	_____
Income before special items (i.e., before discontinued operations, extraordinary items, or cumulative effect)	_____	_____	_____
Net income	_____	_____	_____

   b. From the information in the table above, identify the significant data points or trends that you observe over the three years.

   _____

   _____

   _____

   _____

   _____

_____

_____

_____

_____

_____

_____

_____

_____

_____

_____

_____

_____

_____

_____

_____

7. Summarize your firm's profit margins that you computed in No. 6.a. for each of the last three years.

	Most Recent Year	Next Most Recent Year	Second Most Recent Year
Gross profit margin % (gross margin/sales revenue)	_____	_____	_____
Operating profit margin % (operating income/sales revenue)	_____	_____	_____
Net profit margin % (net income/sales revenue)	_____	_____	_____

8. For perspective, compare your company's profit margins for the most recent year to those computed by classmates for their firms' most recent year.

Alternative

As an alternative to comparing your company's profit margins to those of your classmates, you may want to compare with the companies that you used in No. 3.e. of Assignment 3.

Check with your professor to make sure this alternative is acceptable.

	Your Firm	COMPARATIVE FIRMS				
		Firm 1	Firm 2	Firm 3	Firm 4	Firm 5
Gross profit margin %	____	____	____	____	____	____
Operating profit margin %	____	____	____	____	____	____
Net profit margin %	____	____	____	____	____	____

9. How do your firm's margins correlate to those of your comparative firms? Are they high, low, or about the same? Is there anything specific about your firm, its industry, or your comparative companies or industries that would tend to explain the differences between your company's margins and those of the other firms? Discuss. Also, how would you describe the trend in your company's margins over the past three years?

_____

_____

_____

_____

_____

_____

_____

_____

_____

_____

_____

_____

_____

_____

_____

_____

10. Other common measures of profitability are the *return on assets* and *return on equity*. They are measures of efficiency that compare net income to the amount of assets and equity used to generate that income. The higher the returns, the more efficient was the use of assets and equity.

   a. Compute your firm's return on assets and return on equity for the most recent year using the following formulas.

   Note: *The exact formulas used to compute these ratios vary slightly among financial analysts.*

   $$\text{Return on assets} = \frac{\text{net income}}{\text{average total assets}^*}$$

   $$\text{Return on assets} = \underline{\hspace{3cm}}$$

$$\text{Return on equity} = \frac{\text{net income}}{\text{average stockholders' equity}^*}$$

$$\text{Return on equity} = \underline{\hspace{8cm}}$$

$$^* \quad \frac{\text{beginning balance} + \text{ending balance}}{2}$$

b. Compare your company's returns to those of your comparative firms.

	Your Firm	COMPARATIVE FIRMS				
		Firm 1	Firm 2	Firm 3	Firm 4	Firm 5
Return on assets	____	____	____	____	____	____
Return on equity	____	____	____	____	____	____

c. Assume this year's returns are representative of normal results. Do you think your company is an attractive investment? Discuss.

_____

_____

_____

_____

_____

_____

_____

_____

_____

On the Internet
To compare your company's profits (computed in No. 7) and profitability (computed in No. 10) with your company's industry, visit the Hock homepage at **hock.swlearning.com**, click on "assignments" and follow the instructions for Assignment 6.

Reading 6
EBITDA's Foggy Bottom Line

Reprinted from the January 14, 2003, issue of *Business Week Online* by permission. © 2003 by The McGraw-Hill Companies.

By David Shook in New York

Critics say the accounting method can obscure grim financial realities – and some see AOL Time Warner as the classic example.

Once upon a time, most companies treated revenues, cash flow, and net income as the sacred measures of performance – the numbers on which investors should focus. Then about a decade ago, media and technology outfits adopted their own performance benchmark – a variation on cash flow known as EBITDA, or earnings before interest expense, taxes, depreciation, and amortization. Telecoms followed suit, and over the years the industries that embraced EBITDA began to promote it as a more appropriate measure of earnings than net income.

The rationale behind EBITDA was that it reflects what's happening in core operations, while stripping out expenses that are, in theory, extraneous. The accountants who came up with this idea inevitably worked for companies that took on large amounts of debt to fund acquisitions. They argued that taxes vary so much, depending on acquisitions and losses in prior years, as to distort net income. Moreover, they posited that depreciation of assets which rises in the wake of frequent mergers – doesn't involve any real outflow of cash and, there-fore, shouldn't be allowed to artificially lower profits.

BEAUTIFIED EARNINGS. And what of interest expense on bil-lions of dollars in debt? That doesn't really reflect how a com-pany's sales are going, at least to some accountants. Says James Owers, professor of finance at Georgia State University's Rob-inson College of Business: "EBITDA is what the opera-tional managers hand off to the CFO to pay the taxes and the interest on the debt."

EBITDA "can drift from the realm of reality."

Turns out it's one other thing, too: a vehicle for shifting the attention of investors from a company's overly burdensome debt and chronic charges against earnings. In fact, numerous ac-counting and finance profession-als are suddenly starting to view EBITDA with suspicion, seeing it as a gimmick to dress up earn-ings performance, says Gary J. Previts, an accounting professor at Case Western Reserve Univer-sity in Cleveland. First Call/ Thomson Financial Managing Director Chuck Hill and billion-aire investor Warren Buffett have argued that EBITDA's pri-mary purpose is to pretty up fi-nancial results.

Pamela Stumpp, manager director of Moody's [Mergent's] Investors Service, says emphasis on EBITDA is often misleading because it can overstate cash flow and tell investors little, if anything, about earnings quality while ignoring changes in work-ing capital that might point to a company spending beyond its means. EBITDA "can drift from the realm of reality," says Stumpp, who wrote a widely circulated report on its short-comings in 2000. "It shouldn't be used as the principal determi-nant of cash flow." Yet some companies treat EBITDA as though it should be held in high-er regard than cash flow.

JUST SAY "IBIDDA." Granted, AOL Time Warner (AOL) and others that use EBITDA still re-port parent-company net income and other essential numbers, as required by the Securities & Ex-change Commission. But too often, critics say, they highlight EBITDA as the golden yardstick. AOL Time Warner issues earn-ings guidance only in terms of EBITDA. And it breaks down the performance of each operating unit solely by its EBITDA. AOL Chief Executive Richard Parsons utters the acronym so often in earnings calls that he has devel-oped a fancy way of saying it: "Ibidda."

Investors will hear Parsons say it plenty on Jan. 29. That's when AOL Time Warner reports fourth-quarter results – which, it has already said, should show EBITDA of roughly $8.8 billion in 2002, up about 5% to 6%. That sounds a lot better than the $53 billion net loss AOL is expected to report, vs. its net loss of $4.9 billion in 2001. The huge number for 2002 will reflect a $54 billion writedown based on the excess that AOL paid for Time Warner assets over what they were really worth. Even excluding the outsize noncash charge, AOL had income of only about $927 million – or less than 10% of its EBITDA, according to estimates from CIBC World Markets analyst Michael Gallant.

In 2003, AOL will probably take another writedown of goodwill, this time to reflect the diminished value of its America Online business. Analyst Youssef Squali at First Albany expects this second charge to exceed $10 billion. But that won't show up in AOL's EBITDA estimate for 2003.

MATTERS OF INTEREST. And of course, the EBITDA calculation excludes AOL's huge debt burden, notes Robert Burgoyne, a financial adviser in Ellicott City, Md. With $28 billion in long-term borrowings, AOL Time Warner likely paid more than $1.7 billion in interest in 2002 and could lay out the same amount in 2003. Given that it has interest payments equal to 20% of EBITDA, its favored method for expressing earnings simply ignores one of its largest expenses.

Certainly, it's not illegal to trumpet EBITDA. Hundreds of companies report it, and most investment banks still consider it useful in assessing creditworthiness. "It comes down to a company's right to free speech," says professor Previts. As long as companies disclose all the financial information in the public filings that the SEC requires, they can describe the numbers in press releases and earnings calls any way they choose.

The problem with doing so in AOL Time Warner's case, argues Peter Cohan, an independent financial adviser in Marlborough, Mass., is that EBITDA doesn't reflect what's really happening. "EBITDA is conventional wisdom in the media industry that makes even less sense now than ever," he asserts. AOL declined to comment, though it defends EBITDA in its earnings releases as a valid measure of performance.

That's a position it's free to take – though as criticism of EBITDA mounts, AOL Time Warner's use of it could have the unintended effect of shining an even brighter light into the dark corners of its financial reports.

Business Week Online
www.businessweek.com
January 14, 2003

Questions for Consideration

1. Describe the three earnings measures discussed, i.e., net income, cash flow from operations, and EBITDA. From an investor's perspective, which measure do you believe best portrays a company's true operations? Why?

2. Another measure currently being used to indicate a company's success is *pro forma earnings*—earnings (net income) adjusted for selected items, i.e., any unusual or infrequent charges that management believes distort "real" earnings. Briefly, what similarities are there between EBITDA and pro forma earnings?

Assignment 7
Current Assets and Current Liabilities

Name of your company _____

This assignment focuses on the current asset and current liability sections of the balance sheet and the related notes to the financial statements. Upon completion, you should understand your company's holdings of current assets and current liabilities and how effectively your company is managing them.

Completing the assignment

1. Identify the changes in current asset and current liability accounts that occurred during the most recent accounting period.

Current Assets	Amount on Most Recent Balance Sheet	Amount at End of Prior Year	Net Change in Dollars	in Percent
Cash and cash equivalents	_____	_____	_____	_____
Temporary assets (or short-term investments, or short-term marketable securities)	_____	_____	_____	_____
Accounts receivable, net	_____	_____	_____	_____
Other receivables, net	_____	_____	_____	_____
Inventories	_____	_____	_____	_____
Deferred tax assets	_____	_____	_____	_____
Other _____	_____	_____	_____	_____
Other _____	_____	_____	_____	_____
Total current assets	=======	=======	=======	=====

These two numbers should match the numbers on the balance sheet.

(The assignment continues on the next page.)

Current Liabilities	Amount on Most Recent Balance Sheet	Amount at End of Prior Year	Net Change in Dollars	Net Change in Percent
Accounts payable				
Short-term debt				
Accrued salaries and wages				
Deferred tax liabilities				
Accrued interest				
Current maturities of long-term debt				
Other _____				
Other _____				
Other _____				
Total current liabilities				

These two numbers should match
the numbers on the balance sheet.

2. What significant changes (in amount or percentage) occurred during the most recent year among the current assets and current liabilities? Are any of the changes troubling? Are there any that you might want to investigate further if you were an owner or creditor of your firm? Discuss.

_____

_____

_____

_____

_____

_____

_____

_____

_____

_____

3. Effective management of receivables is critical for most firms. Generally, the change in receivables should be consistent with the change in sales. Provide the following detailed information regarding sales, accounts receivable, and allowance for bad debts (also known as allowance for uncollectible accounts).

   Hint: *Some of this detail may be listed in the notes to the financial statements.*

	End of Most Recent Year	End of Previous Year	Percent Change
a. Sales revenues	_____	_____	_____
b. Gross accounts receivable	_____	_____	_____
c. Less: Allowance for bad debts	_____	_____	_____
d. Net accounts receivable	_____	_____	_____
e. Allowance for bad debts as a percentage of sales	_____	_____	_____
f. Allowance for bad debts as a percentage of ending accounts receivable	_____	_____	_____

g. Are the percentage changes in accounts receivable and allowance for bad debts similar to the change in sales or are they different? Analyze and discuss the meaning or implications of any differences you observe.

_____

_____

_____

_____

_____

_____

_____

_____

_____

_____

_____

_____

4. Effective management of inventory is also critical for most firms. Changes in the levels of inventory should be consistent with changes in the level of cost of goods sold. For example, if the inventory balance increases sharply without a corresponding change in cost of goods sold, it may signal poor inventory management practices or sales expectations that did not materialize. Provide the following detailed information regarding cost of goods sold and the various categories of inventory.

Hint: Some of this detail may be listed in the notes to the financial statements.

Note

Not all firms have inventories. Companies that provide services instead of goods will not have meaningful amounts of inventory. For example, banks, insurance companies, electric power companies and airlines generally do not have meaningful amounts of inventory. As the United States moves to a more service-based economy, there are more and more companies such as Federal Express (package delivery services) and H&R Block (income tax preparation services) that do not have inventory.

If your firm is primarily a service firm without significant amounts of inventory you may skip this section. Ask your professor if he/she wishes you to substitute another firm's data for this section of the assignment.

		End of Most Recent Year	End of Previous Year	Percent Change
a.	Cost of goods sold	_____	_____	_____
b.	Merchandise inventory	_____	_____	_____
c.	Raw materials inventory	_____	_____	_____
d.	Work in process inventory	_____	_____	_____
e.	Finished goods inventory	_____	_____	_____
f.	Other _____	_____	_____	_____
Total inventories		_____	_____	_____
		sum of b, c, d, e, and f		

g. Is the change in total inventories (and the change in each component of inventory) similar to the change in cost of goods sold or different? Discuss the implications of any differences you observe.

_____

_____

_____

_____

_____

_____

_____

_____

_____

5. Which inventory valuation methods are used by your firm? (Mark all that apply.)

   Hint: This information usually is provided in the first note to the financial statements. Service firms probably won't have inventories.

   > **Note**
   > The Dollar-value LIFO, Retail LIFO, and Retail dollar-value LIFO methods listed below are merely specialized applications of the basic LIFO method you have learned about in class. In addition, almost every firm will report that they apply the lower-of-cost-or-market method. This means that the LIFO or FIFO amount does not exceed the cost of replacing the inventory. (As used here, "market" means replacement cost.)

   a. _____ Weighted average

   b. _____ FIFO

   c. _____ LIFO

   d. _____ Dollar-value LIFO

   e. _____ Retail LIFO

   f. _____ Retail dollar-value LIFO

   g. If more than one method is used, does one method predominate?

   _____ Yes   _____ No

   If so, indicate that method. _____

   h. Are inventories reported using lower-of-cost-or-market? _____

   > **Note**
   > The following four ratios provide information about how well a firm manages its current assets and current liabilities.
   >
   > **Current ratio** (also known as the **working capital ratio**) shows how many dollars of current assets are available to pay off each dollar of current liabilities (as of the balance sheet date). This ratio measures liquidity, the ability of a company to pay its bills as they come due.
   >
   > $$\frac{\text{current assets}}{\text{current liabilities}}$$
   >
   > **Quick ratio** (also known as the **acid-test ratio**) is a "tighter" measure of liquidity in that inventory and prepaid expenses are excluded from the numerator.
   >
   > $$\frac{\text{cash} + \text{cash equivalents} + \text{short} \cdot \text{term investments} + \text{accounts receivable}}{\text{current liabilities}}$$

Accounts receivable turnover ratio measures the velocity of receivables through the firm. In general, the faster that receivables are collected the better; the higher the turnover the better.

$$\frac{\text{sales revenue}}{\text{average accounts receivable*}}$$

Inventory turnover ratio is an indicator of how long inventory is held before being sold. A high turnover is favorable and means that inventory is held only a short time before sale.

$$\frac{\text{cost of goods sold}}{\text{average inventory *}}$$

$$\text{* } \frac{\text{beginning balance } + \text{ ending balance}}{2}$$

6. Calculate each of the following ratios for the most recent year available. Enter your results into the first column of the table below. For perspective, compare your firm's ratios for the most recent year to those of your classmates' firms.

Alternative

As an alternative to comparing your company's ratios with those of your classmates' companies, you may want to compare with the companies you used in No. 3.e. of Assignment 3.

Check with your professor to make sure this option is acceptable.

	Your Firm	COMPARATIVE FIRMS				
		Firm 1	Firm 2	Firm 3	Firm 4	Firm 5
a. Current ratio	_____	_____	_____	_____	_____	_____
b. Quick ratio (Acid-test ratio)	_____	_____	_____	_____	_____	_____
c. Accounts receivable turnover ratio	_____	_____	_____	_____	_____	_____
d. Inventory turnover ratio	_____	_____	_____	_____	_____	_____

7. How do your firm's ratios compare to those of your comparative firms? Are they high, low, or about the same? Is there anything specific about your firm, its industry, or your comparative firms or industries that might tend to explain the differences between your company's ratios and those of the other firms? Discuss.

_____

_____

_____

8. Optional Memo No. 2 – Current Assets and Current Liabilities

    Your second memo is based on what you have learned about your company's earnings and current accounts.

    Guide for Memo No. 2

    a. Having studied your company's income statement, discuss why you believe that your company is growing, declining, or remaining constant.

    b. Perhaps the three most significant current accounts related to net income are accounts receivable, inventory, and accounts payable. Do the changes in these accounts appear consistent with your company's earnings pattern? Explain why or why not.

    c. Based on this analysis of your company, would you add it to an equity portfolio? Explain.

Reading 7
Big GAAP and Little GAAP:
Has this idea's time come?

By Glenn Cheney

BATON ROUGE, LA. — The concept has been kicking around for years: the idea of one set of generally accepted accounting principles for big companies, and another for small companies. Or maybe the better division is between public companies and private companies.

Or maybe all companies — from the corner Mom-and-Pop shop to the ponderous multinational conglomerate — should use the same accounting methods, as they always have.

Earlier this year, Barry Melancon, chair and president of the American Institute of CPAs, called for "a very open discussion" over the wisdom and expediency of "differential accounting," the concept that was once termed "Big GAAP-Little GAAP."

"We had this debate in the 1980s and 1990s, and decided against differential accounting," Melancon said. "But the world is a different place today. The biggest public companies are bigger than ever. The complexity of their transactions is more complex, and the gap between them and Joe's Hot Dog Stand is wider today than at any time in history. Therefore, it is legitimate to ask whether the financial reporting model stipulated by the Financial Accounting Standards Board should apply to private businesses."

Melancon pointed out that half of the U.S. economy is generated by non-public companies, and those companies comprise the vast majority of business entities in the country — 15,000 public companies versus uncounted millions of non-public companies.

On the "let's do it" side of the debate is Bill Balhoff, CPA, a partner with the Baton Rouge firm of Postlethwaite & Netterville, a member of the governing Council of the American Institute of CPAs, and a member of the Financial Accounting Standards Advisory Council.

Balhoff says that now the time has come. "The winds have changed," he said. "I've always been of the opinion that if an answer's right, it's the correct answer for everybody, that there was no need for differential accounting. But it has become very questionable whether the generally accepted accounting principles being put out by the Financial Accounting Standards Board are right for non public companies."

As a member of FASAC, which identifies accounting issues that need to be dealt with, Balhoff has formally asked FASB to openly consider separate standards for private companies.

The last straw for Balhoff was FASB's Statement 150. It changed a rule that once let a company — typically a small one — buy back equity from a departing partner and record it as equity. Statement 150 says that the transaction creates a liability. That may be a good rule for large companies, where such a put-back is probably some kind of debt instrument but is not the primary means of capitalizing the company. Applying that principle to a small company that capitalizes itself with partner equity, however, creates a crushing preponderance of liability. The statement, said Balhoff, is a clear indication that FASB wrote the rule without considering it's effect on small companies.

"FASB is working at 50,000 feet, at least," Balhoff said. "They can say what they want; but, in fact, they are writing standards for public companies."

Balhoff also cites the problem of U.S. standards converging with those of the International Accounting Standards Board. International standards are even more oriented to large, multinational corporations. Applying those same standards to Joe's Hot Dog Stand could bury Joe in paperwork, resulting in a severe shortage of local weenies.

Balhoff cites the probable

new rule on accounting for employee stock option compensation as another example. The rule is likely to require a calculation of volatility even if the stock is not traded on the market. If the rule prohibits an assumption of zero volatility, nonpublic companies will have to hire an appraiser every year to value their un-tradeable stock — an onerous and needless expense for a smaller company.

Balhoff said that since FASB is now being funded entirely by public companies, it will be all the more responsive to the demands of the Public Company Accounting oversight Board, the Securities and Exchange Commission, and public companies. He fears that FASB will pay proportionately less attention to smaller companies.

"FASB's concern is going to be over what the PCAOB and SEC are saying and what suits the investors of these large public companies," said Balhoff. "That's a big issue, but let's not ignore the issue of the rest of the companies that have to apply these standards."

Balhoff is talking very big stuff here. Financial accounting standards aren't cranked out overnight. A new set of standards customized for non-public companies would likely have to come from a new standard selling body — perhaps an entity under the Financial Accounting Foundation, which funds and oversees FASB, or a committee within the AICPA. There is also the possibility of a board independent of undue influence from any existing governmental, commercial or professional organization.

Melancon is confident that if

a new entity is created to write a new set of standards, the institute should be the organization that oversees it. The institute's Auditing Standards Board is currently preparing to consider special auditing standards for non public companies. Melancon sees the possibility of a similar structure for accounting standards.

Differential accounting sounds good when you talk about it, but when the alternatives are actually presented to the people who would be asked to follow the new principles, it's never had a lot of traction.

"While the ASB is technically within the AICPA, and we support it, its activities are autonomous," Melancon said. "Our governing council and staff cannot go into the standard-setting body and say, 'You need to make this decision.' The decision is made in the sunshine, through a deliberative process, with exposure and public comment. Our bylaws give us the ability to designate that body and have it serve in the public interest."

At FASB, board member Michael Crooch sees little need for more standards. "My advice would be to be sure this is demand-driven," Crooch said.

"Differential accounting sounds good when you talk about it, but when the alternatives are actually presented to the people who would be asked to follow the new principles, it's never had a lot of traction. The issue has been addressed many times before, but it has never gotten anywhere. It could be — and I don't have any facts — but it could be that the mood of the country has

changed," he said.

John Wulff, chair of Hercules Inc. and a former FASB member who resigned before the end of his term, sees the call for differential reporting as an opportunity. "I think it's appropriate and positive to have a robust dialogue about differential reporting, the pros and cons and the reasons for raising the issue in the first place," Wulff said.

"I would very much like to see the outcome of that dialogue be a commitment from FASB to seize the opportunity for improvement, and come up with standards that are useful to the private and public company sectors. I'm not a believer in differential reporting, but I think private companies are raising issues of cost-benefit and the usefulness of information that the board ought to take a look at," he added.

Balhoff said that slicing out private-company accounting from the purview of FASB would make the board's job easier. Statements would not have to be fashioned to fit companies of all sizes and functions. At the same time, it would become easier to converge with international standards. It might also alleviate one shortcoming of the board — its inability to attract board members and staff from small accounting firms.

On the other hand, a new set of standards would bring its own set of problems.

Auditors would have to learn two kinds of accounting. Educating accountants, auditors and financial analysts would be more difficult. Financial numbers in public and private companies would not be immediately comparable. Private companies going public would need to generate new financial statements. In fact, their current numbers would have to be converted to meet the new principles.

Accounting Today
Nov. 24 - Dec. 14, 2003
Pages 5 and 48

Question for Consideration

The debate between advocates of one GAAP and those supporting a different GAAP for small companies continues. Which side of the debate do you support and why?

Name _____ Professor _____

Course _____ Section _____

Assignment 8
Long-term Assets

Name of your company _____

In this assignment you will review and evaluate the decisions which your company's management has made regarding long-term assets. This includes plant (or fixed) assets, intangible assets, and long-term investments.

Completing the Assignment

1. Identify the changes in your firm's long-term asset accounts that occurred during the most recent accounting period. You will probably have to search the footnotes to obtain some of the specific account information requested. Blank spaces have been provided for you to write in any additional items that appear in your company's Annual Report or SEC 10-K under long-term assets.

Long-term Assets	Amount on Most Recent Balance Sheet	Amount at End of Prior Year	Net Change in Dollars	in Percent
Machinery and equipment				
Building (and leasehold improvements)				
Land				
Other _____				
Other _____				
Other _____				
Less: Accumulated depreciation				
Net* Property, Plant and Equipment				
Construction in progress				
Deferred tax assets				
Long-term receivables				

*Original cost of depreciable assets minus accumulated depreciation to date.

Long-term Assets (cont.)	Amount on Most Recent Balance Sheet	Amount at End of Prior Year	Net Change in Dollars	in Percent
Long-term investments	_____	_____	_____	_____
Excess of cost over net assets of acquired companies, i.e., goodwill	_____	_____	_____	_____
Patents, copyrights, and trademarks	_____	_____	_____	_____
Other _____	_____	_____	_____	_____
Other _____	_____	_____	_____	_____
Total long-term assets	_____	_____	_____	_____

These two numbers should match
the numbers on the balance sheet.

2. Based on the information above, briefly summarize the significant changes in long-term asset accounts, if any, that occurred during the most recent year.

_____

_____

_____

_____

_____

_____

_____

_____

_____

_____

_____

_____

_____

_____

3. Accounting policies related to long-term assets

   Hint: *Most of this information will be found in the first note to the financial statements.*

> ## Note
> The terms depreciation, amortization, and depletion are used to
> indicate very similar processes. All refer to the process of allocat-
> ing part of the cost of a long-term asset to expense.
>
> ▸ When allocating a portion of the cost of tangible fixed assets to
>   expense, accountants use the term *depreciation*.
>
> ▸ When referring to this process for intangible assets, accoun-
>   tants use the term *amortization*.
>
> ▸ When referring to this process for natural resource assets,
>   accountants use the term *depletion*.

a. Depreciation: Which depreciation method(s) does your firm use for financial
   reporting purposes? Check all that apply.

   1) _____ Straight-line

   2) _____ Sum-of-the-year's digits

   3) _____ Declining-balance

   4) _____ Other (specify) _____

   5) If multiple depreciation methods are used, which method is used pre-
      dominantly? _____

   6) Does your firm disclose the estimated useful lives that it assumes for
      depreciating its tangible fixed assets. If yes, describe them.

      _____

      _____

      _____

b. Does your firm report any intangible assets on the balance sheet? If yes,
   describe the policies, e.g., method and estimated life, your firm uses to
   compute amortization expense.

   _____

   _____

   _____

c. Does your firm report any natural resource assets? If yes, describe the
   policies, e.g., method and estimated useful life, your firm uses to compute
   depletion expense.

   _____

   _____

   _____

> **Note**
>
> When one firm controls another firm (such as by owning more than 50% of its voting stock), the second firm is a subsidiary of the first and *consolidated* financial statements are presented.
>
> Consolidated statements combine the financial information of the subsidiaries with that of the parent firm. Use of the term "consolidated" in the title of financial statements indicates that the firm controls at least one other firm.

4. Does your firm own one or more subsidiaries?

   _____ Yes   _____ No

   Hint: Does your firm present "consolidated" financial statements, e.g., consolidated balance sheet, consolidated income statement?

   a. If the answer to No. 4 was yes, determine whether all the subsidiaries are 100% wholly-owned.

   Hint: If any subsidiary is only partially owned, there will be an account listed on the balance sheet (usually after long-term liabilities but before stockholders' equity) with a title something like "Minority Interest." Check one of the following.

   1) _____ All subsidiaries are 100% wholly-owned.

   2) _____ At least one subsidiary is less than 100% wholly-owned.

> **Note**
> In general, when a company owns stock of another firm, but not enough to control the firm, this ownership of shares is accounted for as an "investment" and is reported under long-term assets on the investor company's balance sheet.

   b. Did your firm report any investments in other firms on its balance sheet under the category of long-term investments?

   _____ Yes   _____ No

   c. If yes, inspect the notes to the financial statements to determine which of the following accounting methods are used by your firm to account for this investment(s). Mark all of the following that apply.

   1) _____ Cost method

   2) _____ Market-to-market (or fair value) method

   3) _____ Equity method

d. Did your firm acquire or dispose of any subsidiaries or investments in other firms during the most recent year?

Hint: *This will be discussed in the notes if it occurred. It will probably also show up on the statement of cash flows.*

If yes, describe the acquisitions or disposals that occurred.

_____

_____

_____

_____

_____

_____

_____

_____

_____

_____

_____

_____

Note

The following four ratios provide information about a company's use of long-term assets.

Depreciation and amortization to average long-term assets ratio indicates how rapidly the firm is expensing (writing off) its long-term assets. This can be critical in an industry experiencing rapidly changing technology.

$$\frac{\text{depreciation expense} + \text{amortization expense}}{\text{average long} \cdot \text{term assets}^*}$$

$$^*\frac{\text{current year' s ending balance} + \text{prior year' s ending balance}}{2}$$

Long-term assets to total assets ratio indicates a firm's financial flexibility. The larger the portion of long-term assets, the less flexibility the firm has to change strategies quickly.

$$\frac{\text{long} \cdot \text{term assets}}{\text{total assets}}$$

Plant assets to total assets ratio indicates financial flexibility but focuses only on the investment in land, buildings, equipment, etc.

$$\frac{\text{plant assets}}{\text{total assets}}$$

Sales to average plant assets ratio measures productivity of the plant assets. It shows how many dollars of sales were generated by each dollar invested in plant assets. (How hard are the plant assets working?)

$$\frac{\text{sales}}{\text{average plant assets}^*}$$

$$* \quad \frac{\text{beginning balance} + \text{ending balance}}{2}$$

5. Compute each of the four ratios above for the most recent year and enter the result in the first column below. To give perspective to your results, check with five classmates to determine the value of the ratios for their firms. Record the information below.

Alternative

As an alternative to comparing your company's ratios with those of your classmates' companies, you may want to compare with the companies you used in No. 3.e. of Assignment 3.

Check with your professor to make sure this alternative is acceptable.

		Your Firm	COMPARATIVE FIRMS				
			Firm 1	Firm 2	Firm 3	Firm 4	Firm 5
a.	$\dfrac{\text{deprec. exp.} + \text{amort. exp.}}{\text{average long-term assets}}$	_____	_____	_____	_____	_____	_____
b.	$\dfrac{\text{long-term assets}}{\text{total assets}}$	_____	_____	_____	_____	_____	_____
c.	$\dfrac{\text{plant assets}}{\text{total assets}}$	_____	_____	_____	_____	_____	_____
d.	$\dfrac{\text{sales}}{\text{average plant assets}}$	_____	_____	_____	_____	_____	_____

e. How do your firm's long-term asset ratios compare to those of your comparison firms? Are they high, low, about the same? Is there anything specific about your firm, its industry, or your comparison firms or industries that tend to explain the differences between your company's long-term asset ratios and those of the other firms?

Discuss and explain.

_____

_____

_____

_____

_____

_____

_____

_____

_____

_____

_____

_____

_____

_____

_____

_____

_____

_____

_____

_____

_____

_____

_____

_____

_____

_____

_____

_____

_____

Reading 8
Principles-Based Approach to U.S. Standard Setting

Reprinted with permission from the November 2002 *FASB Report*.
© by Financial Accounting Standards Board, 401 Merritt 7, P.O. Box 5116, Norwalk, CT 06856-5116, U.S.A.

By Linda A. MacDonald
Project Manager

Overview

Recently, many have expressed concerns about the quality and transparency of financial reporting in the United States. In response, the FASB has issued for public comment a proposal for a principles-based approach to U.S. standard setting and plans to hold a public roundtable meeting with respondents to the proposal on December 16. In addition, the Sarbanes-Oxley Act of 2002 requires the Securities and Exchange Commission (SEC) to conduct a study on the adoption of a similar approach and to submit the results of that study to Congress by July 2003.

The Principles

The idea of a principles-based approach to U.S. standard setting is not new. The Board's conceptual framework contains the body of principles that underlies U.S. accounting and reporting. The Board has used the conceptual framework in developing the principles in accounting standards for more than 20 years. However, many assert that the standards have become increasingly detailed and rules-based (with "bright-lines" and "on-off" switches that focus on the form rather than the substance of

transactions), complex, and difficult and costly to apply. Many also assert that the standards allow financial and accounting engineering to structure transactions "around" the rules, referring to situations such as those in which complex structures or a series of transactions are created to achieve desired accounting results; for example, to remove assets from the balance sheet while retaining the overall economics of the assets or to recharacterize assets.

Under a principles-based approach, the principles in accounting standards would continue to be developed from the conceptual framework, but would apply more broadly than under existing standards, thereby providing few exceptions to the principles. In addition, the FASB and other standard-setting bodies would provide less interpretive and implementation guidance for applying the standards. Because exceptions and interpretive and implementation guidance are largely demand-driven, a principles-based approach would require changes in the processes and behaviors not just of the FASB and other standard-setting bodies, but of all participants in the U.S. financial accounting and reporting process-including preparers, auditors, the SEC and users of financial

information. Significant changes are discussed below.

Few, if Any, Exceptions

Exceptions in accounting standards create situations in which the principles in the standards do not apply. Under a principles-based approach, it might not be possible to eliminate all exceptions. However, the Board believes that an objective of that approach should be to eliminate exceptions that are intended to achieve desired accounting results (for example, to limit volatility of reported earnings), which may obscure the underlying economics of the related transactions and events. To achieve that objective, the Board would need to resist pressures to provide exceptions in accounting standards. In turn, others (preparers and users of financial information) would need to accept the consequences of applying accounting standards with fewer exceptions to the principles, including increased volatility in reported earnings.

Implementation of Principles-Based Standards

In addition to the FASB, other standard-setting bodies, including the FASB Emerging Issues Task Force (EITF) and the AICPA Accounting Standards Executive Committee (AcSEC), provide interpretive and implementation guidance for applying accounting standards. A principles-based approach would not eliminate the need for interpretive and implementation guidance. However, the Board believes that an objective of that approach should be to provide interpretive and implementation guidance that focuses only on significant matters addressed in the standards, thereby increasing the need to apply professional judgment in the situations not addressed. In commenting on the proposal, Robert H. Herz, FASB Chairman, explained, "To me, it's a matter of where you start, where you stop and what's your home base. Under a principles-based approach, one starts with laying out the key objectives of good reporting in the subject area and then provides guidance explaining the objective and relating it to some common examples. While rules are sometimes unavoidable and the guidance should be sufficient to enable proper implementation of the principles, the intent is not to try to provide specific guidance or rules for every possible situation. Rather, if in doubt, the reader is directed back to the principles." He added that a principles-based approach, while desirable, would require participants to exercise good professional judgment and "resist the urge to seek specific

answers and rulings on every implementation issue."

To achieve an objective of providing interpretive and implementation guidance that focuses only on significant matters addressed in the standards, the Board and other standard-setting bodies would need to resist pressures to provide interpretive and implementation guidance addressing all possible applications of the standards. In that regard, the Board would need to establish guidelines sufficient to identify situations in which interpretive and implementation guidance in accounting standards is appropriate. To ensure that those (or similar) guidelines are applied consistently after the standards are issued and to improve consistency in establishment of standards, the FASB is taking the lead in realigning the structure of U.S. standard setting. Among other things, the FASB is implementing changes to the roles and processes of the EITF whereby the FASB will have more direct involvement with the agenda, deliberations and conclusions of the EITF. Also, in collaboration with the AICPA, the FASB has proposed that AcSEC cease issuing Statements of Position that create new U.S. GAAP. While the AICPA would continue to issue industry accounting and auditing guides by way of implementation guidance, the FASB

would take on the responsibility for the standard-setting role filled currently by AcSEC.

In any event, preparers and auditors would need to apply professional judgment in more situations. In turn, the SEC and users of financial information would need to accept the consequences of applying professional judgment in more situations, including some divergence in practice.

The Board believes that an approach focusing more clearly on the principles in accounting standards is necessary to improve the quality and transparency of U.S. financial accounting and reporting. Also, a principles-based approach is similar to the approach used by the International Accounting Standards Board (IASB) in developing International Financial Reporting Standards (IFRS). Thus, adopting such an approach could facilitate convergence as the FASB works with the IASB and other national standard setters in developing common high-quality accounting standards. The Board believes that if all participants in the U.S. financial accounting and reporting process are willing to make the changes required under a principles-based approach, the benefits of adopting that approach would outweigh its costs.

Financial Accounting Standards Board
November 27, 2002
Pages 4 - 5

Questions for Consideration

1. Which method of setting accounting standards do you believe is a better approach: *principles-based* or *rules-based*? Why?

2. If the principles-based approach is universally adopted, what potential problems do you foresee? Explain.

Name _____   Professor _____

Course _____   Section _____

Assignment 9
Long-term Liabilities

Name of your company _____

The purpose of this assignment is to understand and evaluate the decisions your company's management has made regarding long-term liabilities.

Key References for this Assignment

1. *Mergent Bond Record*, Mergent FIS, Inc. (a monthly service)

2. *Bond Guide*, Standard & Poor's Corporation, (a monthly service)

Completing the Assignment

1. Identify the changes in the long-term liability accounts that occurred during the most recent accounting period. Blank spaces have been provided for you to write in additional items that appear in your firm's long-term liability section.

Long-term Liabilities	Amount on Most Recent Balance Sheet	Amount at End of Prior Year	Net Change in Dollars	in Percent
Long-term debt	_____	_____	_____	_____
Capitalized lease obligations	_____	_____	_____	_____
Deferred tax liabilities	_____	_____	_____	_____
Pension liability	_____	_____	_____	_____
Other _____	_____	_____	_____	_____
Total long-term liabilities	_____	_____	_____	_____

These two numbers should match
the numbers on the balance sheet.

2. Based on the information in No. 1 and that found in the notes to the financial statements, briefly summarize the significant changes, if any, in the long-term liability accounts during the most recent year.

_____

_____

_____

_____
_____
_____
_____
_____
_____
_____
_____
_____
_____

3. What are the approximate interest rates incurred on your firm's long-term liabilities? Complete the schedule below. Some items, e.g., deferred tax liabilities, do not incur interest. Some (or most) of this information will be found in the notes to the financial statements.

Long-term Liability Accounts	Approximate Rate of Interest
_____	_____ %
_____	_____ %
_____	_____ %
_____	_____ %
_____	_____ %
_____	_____ %

4. What amount of cash is the firm obligated to pay out in each of the next five years for repayment of long-term debt, capitalized lease obligations, operating leases, and/or other commitments?

Hint: _This information usually is contained in the notes to the financial statements and will take careful reading to identify._

Year	Repayment of Long-term Debt	Capital Lease Obligations	Operating Leases	Other Commitments
Year 1	_____	_____	_____	_____
Year 2	_____	_____	_____	_____
Year 3	_____	_____	_____	_____
Year 4	_____	_____	_____	_____
Year 5	_____	_____	_____	_____
Totals	==========	==========	==========	==========

5. Go to the statement of cash flows. Observe the amount of "net cash flow from operations" generated in each of the last three years. To what extent does it appear that the company will be able to pay off the above scheduled obligations each year with cash generated from operations? Might the company need to raise the required cash in some other way? Discuss.

_____

_____

_____

_____

_____

_____

_____

6. Find and read the footnote about your firm's pension plan(s). Then answer the following questions.

   a. Which type(s) of pension plan does your firm have? Check all that apply. The firm may have either type of plan, both, or none.

   _____ Defined contribution plan

   _____ Defined benefit plan

   _____ None

   b. Fill in the blanks below to determine if your company has sufficient assets to satisfy its pension obligations.

      1) Fair value of pension plan assets   _____

         Less: accumulated benefit obligation (ABO)   – _____

         Excess (deficiency) of plan assets over ABO   = _____

      2) Fair value of pension plan assets   _____

         Less: projected benefit obligation (PBO)   – _____

         Excess (deficiency) of plan assets over PBO   = _____

Note

The accumulated benefit obligation (ABO) is the present value of all pension benefits that employees have earned to date based on their *current* wage rates.

The projected benefit obligation (PBO) is the present value of all pension benefits that employees have earned to date based on their *expected* wage rates at the time they retire.

---

c. If the company were liquidated today, would there be enough pension plan assets for the firm to meet its obligations to its employees? Explain.

Hint: *Focus on the ABO.*

_____

_____

_____

_____

_____

d. If you acquired the company and its employees today, are there enough pension plan assets to cover benefits earned-to-date when the employees retire at their normal retirement dates? Explain.

Hint: *Focus on the PBO.*

_____

_____

_____

_____

_____

_____

7. Identify the investment characteristics of your firm's long-term debt. Obtain the most recent monthly issue of either *Mergent Bond Record* or *Standard & Poor's Bond Guide*. (Companies are listed alphabetically in both publications, but if you have a choice, *Mergent Bond Record* is a little easier to use.) Look up your company to determine whether it has any long-term debt listed, and if so, answer each of the following questions. (If your firm has more than three issues, select three representative issues for listing here.)

	Long-term Debt Issue #1	Long-term Debt Issue #2	Long-term Debt Issue #3
a. Type of debt (Notes, subordinated notes, senior notes, debentures, etc.)	_____	_____	_____
b. Interest rate	_____	_____	_____
c. Year debt is due	_____	_____	_____
d. Debt rating (indicate which rating source you used)			
_____ Mergent	_____	_____	_____
_____ S&P	_____	_____	_____

e. Indicate whether the issue is "investment grade" (rated Baa/BBB or higher) or "speculative grade" ("junk bonds").

	Long-term Debt Issue #1	Long-term Debt Issue #2	Long-term Debt Issue #3
	_____	_____	_____

If your company has no bonds rated by Mergent or S&P, skip to No. 8.

f. Call date of the
    debt, if any   _____   _____   _____

g. Call price of the
    debt, if any   _____   _____   _____

h. Current market
    price   _____   _____   _____

i. Recent price range

    Highest price   _____   _____   _____

    Lowest price   _____   _____   _____

j. Yield to maturity   _____   _____   _____

8. Did your firm disclose any contingencies, sometimes called contingent liabilities, in the notes to the financial statements? Discuss the specific nature of these contingencies and how (or whether) they are expected to affect the firm's financial health.

_____

_____

_____

_____

_____

_____

_____

_____

_____

_____

_____

_____

_____

> ### Note
> The following two ratios are computed to provide information about how a company is managing its long-term liabilities.
>
> **Debt to total assets ratio** reveals the percentage of assets financed by debt. The use of debt financing is referred to as financial leverage. The higher the degree of financial leverage, the higher the risk that a company will not be able to meet its interest payments and will be forced into bankruptcy.
>
> $$\frac{\text{total liabilities}}{\text{total assets}}$$
>
> **Times interest earned ratio** measures the cushion a company has regarding its ability to pay interest charges on its debt. The higher the cushion, the more likely the company will be able to meet its interest payments.
>
> $$\frac{\text{*net income } + \text{ [interest expense (1 - tax rate)]}}{\text{interest expense}}$$
>
> *Many companies report a number on the income statement using the title *operating income*. This amount is often used in the numerator of this ratio instead of the more complex computation shown above. If your company reports *operating income*, use it in the numerator of this ratio.

9. Calculate each of the following ratios for the most recent year using the computational formulas just explained.

    a. Debt to total assets $= \dfrac{\text{total liabilities}}{\text{total assets}}$

    Debt to total assets $= \underline{\hspace{4cm}} = \underline{\hspace{2cm}}\%$

    b. Times interest earned $= \dfrac{\text{net income } + \text{ [interest expense (1 - tax rate)]}}{\text{interest expense}}$

    Times interest earned $= \underline{\hspace{5cm}} = \underline{\hspace{2cm}}$

10. Enter your results into the first column of the table on the next page. For perspective, compare your firm's ratios for the most recent year to those of your classmates' firms.

    ### Alternative

    As an alternative to comparing your company's ratios to those of your classmates' companies, you may want to compare with the companies you used in

No. 3.e. of Assignment 3.

Check with your professor to make sure this option is acceptable.

	Your Firm	COMPARATIVE FIRMS				
		Firm 1	Firm 2	Firm 3	Firm 4	Firm 5
a. Debt to total assets	_____	_____	_____	_____	_____	_____
b. Times interest earned	_____	_____	_____	_____	_____	_____

11. How do your firm's ratios compare to those of your comparative firms? Are they high, low, about the same? Is there anything specific about your firm, its industry, or your comparative firms or industries that might tend to explain the differences between your company's ratios and those of the other firms? Discuss.

_____

_____

_____

_____

_____

_____

_____

_____

_____

_____

_____

_____

_____

_____

_____

_____

_____

_____

_____

_____

_____

_____

_____

Reading 9
Revlon Moves to Relieve Cash Crisis

By Sally Beatty and
Aaron Lucchetti

After months of uncertainty, Revlon Inc. unveiled a debt-for-equity swap and related agreements that will reduce its debt by about 50%, alleviating a cash crisis that has plagued the cosmetics giant.

The rescue package, which includes slashing the company's $1.9 billion debt load by at least $930 million, received the approval of one of Revlon's biggest bondholders, **Fidelity Investments**' Fidelity Management & Research Co., which will exchange $155 million in debt for equity in Revlon. Fidelity also gets two seats on Revlon's 10-member board. Securing Fidelity's commitment is a victory for Revlon in its battle to remove the specter of a bankruptcy filing that has haunted the company for more than a year.

The plan, which calls for issuance of a yet-to-be determined number of additional shares, will reduce the equity stake held by Ronald O. Perelman's **MacAndrews & Forbes Holdings** Inc., which currently has an 83% interest in Revlon. Even so, "we would anticipate and fully expect Ronald to remain the principal shareholder in the company," Revlon Chief Executive Jack Stahl said. Because it is still unclear if other investors will follow Fidelity's lead, it's too early to say how many additional shares Revlon may issue.

The plan will offer big bondholders 300 to 400 shares for every $1,000 in notes tendered for exchange. Revlon said it expects $780 million in debt to be swapped for equity in the first quarter. MacAndrews & Forbes, Mr. Perelman's main investment vehicle, has agreed to swap $475 million in debt it holds for equity, and has agreed to "backstop" another $300 million in debt if other investors pass on the offer. The backstop covers a $150 million debt-for-equity offer being made available to existing unsecured bondholders in the first quarter, and a rights offering to be completed before the end of this year. MacAndrews will also cover an additional $100 million equity offering scheduled to take place by March 2006, if need be. "This is extremely good news for bondholders," said Brendan White, senior portfolio manager at **Touchstone High-Yield Bond Fund**, which has about 1.2% of its assets, or $1 million, invested in Revlon debt. "This goes a long way to righting the capital structure. Previously, we had to focus on the balance sheet." Now, the company can "focus on improving the business."

Revlon, which has reported a string of quarterly losses, has been struggling to compete in a soft market for cosmetics sold through mass merchants and drug and grocery store chains against bigger and better-funded competitors such as **L'Oreal** SA and **Procter & Gamble** Co. In addition, consumers have been more willing to increase their spending on prestige cosmetics sold in department stores, where Revlon brands aren't distributed.

Yesterday, Revlon released better-than-expected fourth-quarter results, surprising some company watchers. In the quarter, Revlon narrowed its loss to $12.6 million, or 18 cents a share, compared with a year-earlier loss of $179.4 million, or $3.36 a share. Sales climbed 73% to $368.5 million from $212.6 million a year earlier. Excluding the company's growth-plan-related returns and allowances, net sales were up 26%, the company said. Revlon attributed the stronger results to sharply lower costs to cover returns from retailers of unsold merchandise, strong consumer response to new products such as its ColorStay Overtime lipstick, licensing revenue and favorable foreign-currency translation.

Deutsche Bank Securities analyst George S. Chalhoub questioned whether the improved results reflected any delays or cuts in discounts, allowances or other brand-support expenses, such as advertising. In an interview, Mr. Stahl said the results "reflect all the things we are doing to grow the business, which are indeed sustainable."

A spokeswoman for Fidelity, Sarah Friedell, said the firm agreed to the debt-for-equity offer because "we believe this is in the best interest of all Revlon shareholders long-term, and our own shareholders."

It remains to be seen whether investors will embrace the offer. Revlon has not yet begun "formal conversations" with other investors, Mr. Stahl said. He added that while the company expects more debt holders to convert their holdings to equity, "the important thing is that the plan is not dependent on additional debt being exchanged by other public owners."

Mr. White said he hadn't decided whether his fund would participate in the debt-for-equity exchange or the other offerings Revlon announced yesterday. Revlon's 8.125% notes due 2006 were trading at 101½ cents yesterday afternoon, up from 75 cents on the dollar on Wednesday, according to Merrill Lynch. Revlon's 8.625% notes, due in 2008, surged even more– to 93 cents from 57 cents on the dollar.

Stock investors were less enthusiastic, sending the shares sharply lower in heavy trading. The stock fell 35 cents, or 9.9%, to $3.19 in 4 p.m. New York Stock Exchange composite trading. "A lot of new shares are coming out," reducing the value of existing shareholders' stakes, said Mr. White. He added, however, that the restructuring "is good for the company," because "it gives them flexibility."

The Wall Street Journal
February 13, 2004
Pages A3 and A5

Questions for Consideration

1. After the debt-for-equity swap announcement, the bond market reacted favorably by increasing the value of Revlon's bond debt, but the stock market reacted by lowering Revlon's market price per share. Why would the bond market and stock market react in opposite ways to the same announcement?

2. Explain how the debt-for-equity swap affects Revlon's capital structure. What other effects will the swap have on Revlon?

Name _____   Professor _____

Course _____   Section _____

Assignment 10
Stockholders' Equity

Name of your company _____

When you have completed this assignment, you should have a thorough understanding of the equity financing activities that your company has engaged in, both during the current period and over its life. Use the information in your firm's annual report to Stockholders and its SEC 10-K Report to complete this assignment. In addition, you will need to consult the most recent issue of *The Wall Street Journal* or the Sunday edition of your local newspaper.

Completing the Assignment

1. Identify the categories and amounts of your firm's capital stock. Some companies have more than one class of common stock, e.g., Class A common and Class B common. Similarly, some companies have more than one issue of preferred stock. Complete the following table for each class of your firm's common stock and each class of your firm's preferred stock. Clearly identify each class of stock and indicate the number of shares in 000's.

Common stock	Authorized	Issued	Outstanding	Par Value (or Stated Value) Per Share
_____	_____	_____	_____	_____
_____	_____	_____	_____	_____
_____	_____	_____	_____	_____

Preferred stock (if any)

_____	_____	_____	_____	_____
_____	_____	_____	_____	_____
_____	_____	_____	_____	_____

2. Identify the changes in your firm's equity accounts that occurred during the most recent accounting period. Not all firms will have an entry for each item while some companies will have items that are not listed here.

Equity accounts	Amount on Most Recent Balance Sheet	Amount at End of Prior Year	Net Change in Dollars	in Percent
Preferred stock	_____	_____	_____	_____
Common stock	_____	_____	_____	_____
Additional paid-in capital (excess over par)	_____	_____	_____	_____
Deferred compensation	_____	_____	_____	_____
Other comprehensive income	_____	_____	_____	_____
Retained earnings	_____	_____	_____	_____
Treasury stock	_____	_____	_____	_____
Other _____	_____	_____	_____	_____
Total stockholders' equity	═══════	═══════	═══════	═════

These two numbers should match
the totals on the balance sheet.

3. Briefly summarize the *significant* changes in stockholders' equity, if any, that occurred during the most recent year.

_____

_____

_____

_____

_____

_____

_____

4. _____ Check here if your firm had no preferred stock outstanding.

   If your company had preferred stock outstanding at any time during the most recent year, indicate which of the following features apply.

	Yes	No	
a.	_____	_____	Cumulative
b.	_____	_____	Participating
c.	_____	_____	Redeemable
d.	_____	_____	Convertible
e.	_____	_____	Voting privileges

f. For characteristics a. through e. that apply to your firm's preferred stock, indicate the specifics of that characteristic to your stock. For example, if it is convertible, under what terms can it be converted?

   Hint: Most of this information will be in the notes.

   _____

   _____

   _____

   _____

   _____

   _____

   _____

5. Indicate below whether your firm had treasury stock at the end of the current period and/or at the end of the prior period.

	Current Balance Sheet	Prior Balance Sheet	Percent Change
a. Number of shares	_____	_____	_____
b. Dollar amount	_____	_____	_____
c. Is it reported at its cost? (If not, ignore d.)	_____	_____	_____
d. What was the average price* paid to acquire the treasury stock?	_____	_____	_____

   $$* \text{ average price } = \frac{\text{total cost}}{\text{number of shares}}$$

6. Did your company issue stock, either common or preferred, during the most recent year?

   Hint: This is reported on the statement of stockholders' equity if one is included in the financial statements. Otherwise, look on the statement of cash flows under Financing Activities and/or on a supplementary schedule that sometimes accompanies the statement of cash flows.

   _____ Yes

   _____ No

   If yes, identify the number of shares issued of each type of stock, par value (if any), and total dollar amount received from each issue.

Type of Stock	Number of Shares Issued	Par Value (Per Share)	Total Dollar Amount
a. _____	_____	_____	_____
b. _____	_____	_____	_____
c. _____	_____	_____	_____
d. _____	_____	_____	_____

7. Does your firm have any executive stock options outstanding at its most recent balance sheet date?

   _____

   If yes, by what percent would the number of common shares outstanding increase if all executive stock options were exercised? Show your clearly labeled work in the space provided below.

   _____ %

Note

The following three ratios are computed to provide information about a company's common stock price and about the company's dividend practices. The computational formula and the information content of each ratio is explained below.

Price-earnings ratio (P/E ratio) measures investors' expectations about a company's future earnings. If investors are paying a high price for the stock, this indicates that they expect significant growth in future earnings and the P/E ratio will be high, e.g., in the 30s or higher. If investors will only pay a low price for the stock, they are indicating pessimism about future earnings growth and the P/E ratio will be low, e.g., in single digits.

$$\frac{\text{current market price of common stock}}{\text{diluted earnings per share}}$$

Dividend payout ratio reveals the percentage of the income earned by the common stock that was paid out in common dividends. In other words, it yields the portion of earnings per share that is paid out as dividends.

$$\frac{\text{total cash dividends paid on common stock}}{\text{net income minus preferred dividends}}$$

Dividend yield ratio ratio measures the cash return per share of common stock. (Note that the *total return* on a share of stock would include both the cash dividend plus or minus the change in the market price of the share.)

$$\frac{\text{cash dividend per share of common stock}}{\text{market price per share of common stock}}$$

8. Compute your firm's price-earnings ratio.

   a. price earnings ratio $= \dfrac{\text{current market price of common stock}}{\text{diluted earnings per share}}$

   price earnings ratio $= \underline{\hspace{4cm}} = \underline{\hspace{3cm}}$

Note

The current market price of your firm's common stock can be obtained from the most recent issue of *The Wall Street Journal* (published every weekday and available in most libraries). You will find the stock prices in Section C. Alternatively, the Sunday edition of most local newspapers carry a summary of end-of-the-week corporate stock prices.

On the Internet

Numerous financial web sites, including many companies, have up-to-date stock quotations. If you need help finding your company's current stock price, go to the Hock homepage at **hock.swcollege.com**, select "assignments," and utilize the links for Assignment 10.

---

   b. Based on the Note about P/E ratios, what does your firm's price-earnings ratio tend to indicate about investors' expectations regarding the company's future earnings?

   _____

   _____

   _____

_____
_____
_____
_____
_____
_____
_____

9. Compute your firm's dividend payout ratio.

   a. dividend payout ratio $= \dfrac{\text{total cash dividends on common stock}}{\text{net income minus preferred dividends}}$

   dividend payout ratio $= \overline{\hspace{5cm}} = \underline{\hspace{3cm}}$

   b. Assuming the dividend payout ratio you just computed has been fairly constant over recent years, briefly explain what this implies about the company's dividend payment policy.

_____
_____
_____
_____
_____
_____
_____

10. Compute your firm's dividend yield ratio.

   a. dividend yield ratio $= \dfrac{\text{cash dividend per share of common stock}}{\text{current market price per share of common stock}}$

   dividend yield ratio $= \overline{\hspace{5cm}} = \underline{\hspace{3cm}}$

   b. Assuming the dividend yield ratio you just computed has been fairly constant over recent years, briefly explain what this reveals about the cash return an owner receives on his/her investment each year. Do you believe this is a satisfactory return on a stockholder's investment? What other source of return (besides dividends) do stockholders earn on their investment?

_____

_____

_____

_____

_____

_____

_____

_____

_____

_____

_____

11. Your third memo is based on your company's investing (long-term assets) and financing (debt and equity) activities.

Guide for Memo No. 3

a. What can you conclude about your company's investing policies? Discuss, using ratios when appropriate.

b. What can you conclude about your company's financing activities? Discuss, using ratios when appropriate.

c. What new insights do you have relative to your assessment of your company? Discuss whether or not you are now more favorably impressed with your company.

Reading 10
Tell the Truth, Unless It Hurts

Reprinted with permission from *The CPA Journal*, September 2003.

By Raymond L. Dever, CPA
(Retired)

Personal Viewpoint

Tell the truth, unless it hurts—or unless it's politically dangerous. "We can't stand by and let accountants wearing green eyeshades decide who is going to get the American dream," said Senator Barbara Boxer (D-Calif.) before a Silicon Valley lobbying organization. And, in a letter jointly written with 14 other senators, Senator Mike Enzi (R-Wyo.) said that FASB's procedures are "seriously flawed" and it should "back up a step and do the critical thinking and analysis that we should expect" before changing the rules. The letter further says that a rule which would require companies to deduct stock option costs from earnings would "eviscerate" compensation plans that distribute options to all employees. These statements were provoked by FASB's decision to consider adding stock option accounting (yet again) to its agenda.

Since then, FASB has decided to do so, and I applaud and fully support that decision. If, however, FASB had decided not to address this issue, I would have understood: It would have been because of the concern over a repeat of the political pressure FASB faced when the issue was last debated in the mid-1990s.

That debate resulted in a compromise that required only the disclosure of options, rather than proper accounting. Now that FASB has decided to revisit the topic, we will again see significant political pressure brought to bear to keep FASB from changing the current antiquated accounting rules.

Senator Enzi says "do the critical thinking." I cannot think of any accounting subject that has been thought about critically more than stock option accounting. Moreover, unlike many legitimate debates on accounting issues, I've never heard an accountant convincingly support, on the merits of the accounting, the current rules. Rather, the Senator's comments are nothing more than another threat, and a thinly veiled one at that.

In no way do I mean to speak disrespectfully of the FASB members who reached the "compromise" the last time. I believe they did the only practical thing at the time, in the face of Congressional leaders and others who threatened to put them out of business: Because of this pressure, the SEC even gave up its support of this much-needed rule change. Why the pressure? High-tech (and other) companies said they liked the current rule, which was written in 1972 and was itself a compromise. (I admit that most accounting firms also supported this

view.) The companies said the current rule worked because it was understood, it had served the public well for many years, and it was simple to apply.

But not so! First, it was not well understood. In fact, only a few professionals in the national offices of large accounting firms really understood it. It was so well understood that in 2000 the FASB issued an interpretation to assist understanding and to curb abuses. Did this guidance—the longest interpretation FASB has ever issued—make the rule understood? No. FASB's Emerging Issues Task Force (EITF) has since had to consider and conclude on more than 50 implementation issues regarding this interpretation.

Second, the rule had not served the public well. It encouraged companies to develop stock option plans for their executives which were less economical for companies and their current stockholders. Those plans often led to executives realizing significant increases in wealth for reasons that had little if anything to do with their efforts.

Last, the rule was not simple to apply. The only simple thing about the rule was the real reason companies wanted to maintain it: to avoid recording a major expense in their income statements.

If these companies had to record as an expense in their

income statements the cost of the options given to employees (this being in many cases a very significant part of employee compensation), they feared their stock price would drop. Is this a reason to mislead current investors by not recording a significant cost of doing business? No. A changed stock option accounting rule, requiring that the options be measured and recorded as an expense in the income statement, would only allow investors to see what management has given to the employees. The investors have a right to know; it's their company.

In the mid-1990s, these companies made these arguments and prevailed because of the political support they were able to attract. Now, when Congress is increasingly scrutinizing and criticizing accounting, these politicians should switch sides or, better yet, stay out of it.

It would seem that Congress would be compelled by its own words and actions to fully support FASB in changing the rules for stock option accounting, but I doubt that that will happen. Rather, now that FASB has courageously decided to engage in the battle to change the rules, I expect that it will continue to face the wrath of those who are content to not tell the truth when it hurts (the companies) or when it is politically dangerous (the politicians). Indeed, Senator Enzi and 12 other senators wrote a letter to the SEC in March, requesting that the SEC undertake a study to examine footnote disclosures to determine the accuracy of the disclosed valuations that were performed using the Black-Scholes valuation method—an exercise I believe is impossible. The politicians are trying to stop the much-needed change to the rules by arguing that the Black-Scholes valuation method is inaccurate. They even suggest the method could be "precisely wrong." Yet it is the method often used by companies in setting the value of compensation packages for their executives. It may not be perfect, and I would support research to develop a better method, but not at the cost of delaying change. The only approach that is precisely wrong is the current rules for stock option accounting.

I would expect nothing different from the companies; they view the continuing misstatement of their income as a survival measure. Very disappointing, however, are the politicians. These are the same politicians that criticize accounting standards setters for not developing standards that lead to fair financial reporting, and that criticize auditors for not standing up to inappropriate pressures from their clients. I see much of the same thing going on here. Enzi and the other senators end their letter to the SEC by stating, "[I]nvestor protection now demands that the SEC undertake this important research to ensure that any decision-making by the FASB is based on an impartial review of all the facts." I guess so. Shame on them.

Author's Note: Since I wrote this article, much of what I predicted has come true. Bills have been introduced in Congress and FASB has been attacked by many for doing what is the only right thing to do if Americans truly want better financial reporting. Fortunately, some prominent persons have supported FASB, and many stockholders have started to focus on this issue and have started to raise concerns. Politicians should realize those stockholders also are constituents. Well, only time will tell.

The CPA Journal
September 2003
Pages 8 - 9

Questions for Consideration

1. Many executives currently receive stock options as part of their compensation package. Do you believe that the cost of the stock options should be included in the determination of net income? Why or why not?

2. For years accounting standards have been set in the private sector. Now politicians (public sector) are pressing for standards that are favorable to their constituents. Should those serving in Congress be able to pressure the FASB to write a standard in a particular way? Explain.

Name _____   Professor _____

Course _____   Section _____

Assignment 11
Segment Information

Name of your company _____

Most large publicly-traded companies have operations in more than one line of business, or operate in various geographic areas, or have different parts of the business subject to differing levels of regulation. The purpose of this assignment is to understand the component parts (segments) of your company's operations. Are some segments growing more rapidly than others? Which are generating most of the company's sales and profits?

To help financial statement users make better judgments about the company as a whole, GAAP require that companies split out certain specific information by segment. To meet these disclosure requirements, firms usually organize their financial results into two, three, or four segments. Seldom does a company report more than five segments. Usually this information is reported near the end of the notes section. In this assignment you will focus primarily on segment revenues, segment assets, and segment profit.

Note
Some firms report that they operate as a single segment. If this is the situation for your firm, you will not be able to complete this assignment. Ask your professor if he/she would like you to use a different company for this part of the **FRP**.

Completing the Assignment

1. Find and read your firm's segment information in the notes to the financial statements. (It's usually one of the last notes.) What is the basis your firm has chosen upon which to report segments? Mark one below.

    _____ Products or services

    _____ Geography

    _____ Regulatory environment

    _____ Type of customer

    _____ Other _____

2. What are the names of your firm's segments and what are the primary types of products that are sold in each? Complete the table below.

Segment Name	Types of Products Sold
a.	
b.	
c.	
d.	
e.	
f.	

3. To determine whether management is "growing" one or more of the segments faster than the others, complete the following table by using the data provided in the notes. Divide (1) the segment's total expenditures for long-term assets by (2) the segment's total assets. Do this for each segment for up to three years.

Total expenditures for long-term assets ÷ total assets

Segment Name	Most Recent Year	Next Most Recent Year	Second Most Recent Year
a. _____	_____ %	_____ %	_____ %
b. _____	_____ %	_____ %	_____ %
c. _____	_____ %	_____ %	_____ %
d. _____	_____ %	_____ %	_____ %
e. _____	_____ %	_____ %	_____ %
f. _____	_____ %	_____ %	_____ %

4. Does your analysis in No. 3. indicate that management is "growing" one or more segments more rapidly than the others? Why might this be? Discuss.

_____

_____

_____

_____

_____

_____

5. Complete the table of segment information below. List the segment profit, segment assets, and return on segment assets (of each segment) for the most recent year and two prior years. List the most recent year's information first. Divide column A by column B to obtain the return on segment assets.

Segment Names	Year	A ÷ Segment Profit	B = Segment Assets	Return on Segment Assets
a. _____	___	___	___	___
	___	___	___	___
	___	___	___	___
b. _____	___	___	___	___
	___	___	___	___
	___	___	___	___
c. _____	___	___	___	___
	___	___	___	___
	___	___	___	___
d. _____	___	___	___	___
	___	___	___	___
	___	___	___	___
e. _____	___	___	___	___
	___	___	___	___
	___	___	___	___
f. _____	___	___	___	___
	___	___	___	___
	___	___	___	___

6. Discuss the results of your segment profitability analysis and include the following.

▸ What trends do you observe?

▸ Are some segments performing better than others?

▸ What segment-related questions would you ask of management if you had the opportunity?

▸ Might overall profitability be enhanced by reallocating assets to some segments and away from others?

▸ Does management address "segment strategies" in the Management Discussion and Analysis section of the Annual Report? What do they say? Discuss and explain.

Note

To better understand profit results, analysts often split return on assets into two component parts: profit margin and asset turnover.

1. The *profit margin* reveals the number of pennies out of each sales dollar that a company retains (as profit) after paying all of its expenses.

$$\text{segment profit margin} = \frac{\text{segment profit}}{\text{total segment revenues}}$$

2. *Asset turnover* reveals how many times during the accounting period that those pennies were earned.

$$\text{segment asset turnover} = \frac{\text{total segment revenues}}{\text{segment assets}}$$

Ideally, companies would prefer to have high profit margin **and** high asset turnover. In reality, companies vary widely in their combinations of margin and turnover. Similarly, segments can vary widely in their margins and turnover. A segment's profit margin multiplied by its asset turnover equals the return on segment assets for that segment.

return on segment assets = segment profit margin × segment asset turnover

---

7. To understand more about how your company's segment profits are generated, compute the profit margin, asset turnover, and return on segment assets for each of your firm's segments. Use the formulas from the Note above for your computations of each segment's profit margin, asset turnover, and return on segment assets.

Segment Name	Segment Profit Margin $\frac{\text{segment profit}}{\text{total segment revenues}}$	×	Segment Asset Turnover $\frac{\text{total segment revenues}}{\text{segment assets}}$	=	Return on Segment Assets
a. _____	_____		_____		_____
b. _____	_____		_____		_____
c. _____	_____		_____		_____
d. _____	_____		_____		_____
e. _____	_____		_____		_____
f. _____	_____		_____		_____

8. Discuss the comparative profit margins and asset turnover that you computed for your company's segments. Do they differ markedly or they all about the same? If there are significant differences, is there anything about the nature of the various products in the different segments that would tend to explain the differences you found? Discuss.

_____

_____

_____

_____

_____

_____

_____

_____

_____

_____

_____

_____

_____

_____

_____

_____

_____

_____

_____

_____

_____

_____

_____

_____

_____

_____

_____

_____

Reading 11
Don't Forget the Fine Print

Reprinted from *Fortune*, June 23, 2003. © Time Inc. All rights reserved.

By Herb Greenberg
Senior columnist, TheStreet.com

If you fail to read the footnotes in a company's filings, you're not getting the whole story.

I recently bought an earthquake policy on my home and was astounded when I read the fine print to see what wouldn't be covered. I bought the policy anyway, and even paid more for a lower deductible. But at least I know what I bought, which is more than I can say for investors—especially when I see stocks going up without regard for their fundamentals.

That is why it's too bad Michele Leder's book *Financial Fineprint, Uncovering a Company's True Value* (John Wiley & Sons, $29.95) won't be in bookstores until August. If ever there were a time investors needed to be reminded about what they own, it's now. Trouble is, the best stuff is often buried deeper than most investors care to dig. "While accounting rules require companies to provide details about how they arrive at many of the key numbers that investors tend to focus on," Leder writes, "there's nothing that requires them to make this easy to find. As a result, most of these details are buried in the footnotes"—or in the Notes to the Consolidated Financial Statements, as they're officially called in annual and quarterly filings

with the SEC.

So which footnotes are the most important? All of them, though at some companies certain footnotes require a closer look than others. For example, at an acquisitive firm like School Specialty, a roll-up of school-supply companies, the footnote on Business Combinations and Proforma Results is a must-read for investors interested in the quality of earnings growth. This footnote shows that in last year's third fiscal quarter, revenues fell by 1% without acquisitions—a much different figure from the 6% rise over the same quarter a year earlier cited in the company's press release. The difference suggests that the company could be reliant on acquisitions for growth. Indeed, the company's own guidance for organic growth since last November has been 0% to 2%, and recent press releases concede that revenue increases have been "driven primarily by acquired businesses."

Another favorite, especially at companies with large insider ownership, is the note on related-party transactions. Take the case of Rollins, which owns the Orkin Exterminating Co. In its 10-K, the company discloses a bevy of relationships involving Rollins and companies owned by chairman Randall Rollins and his brother Gary Rollins, the CEO. But not to worry: According to the same filing, "It is the opinion

of management that these related party transactions ... will not have a material effect on the company's financial position." (Perhaps, but keep in mind that management owns more than half the outstanding shares.)

A smorgasbord of information is contained in a single note called Significant Accounting Policies, which is usually the first or second of all footnotes. That is where a company discloses many of the nuts and bolts of its approach to accounting, including revenue recognition, a key ingredient to determining earnings quality. Of special note is when a company uses a less conservative method of accounting than many of its peers. Texas Instruments, for example, discloses that it books revenue when a product is shipped to distributors. The trouble with booking revenue that way, critics claim, is that distributors might be coerced into taking more products than they can reasonably sell, thereby inflating sales. A spokeswoman for Texas Instruments, however, responds that TI believes that booking sales sold to distributors "adds integrity to our accounting data" because it doesn't have to wait until distributors report back with sales figures. Plenty of companies do the same, but quite a few others, including Intel, wait until distributors sell the products to end-customers. Intel's reason, included in its

10-K: Chips are subject to "frequent sales price reductions and rapid technology obsolescence."

Beyond the actual footnotes, investors can also find plenty of nifty data in the Management's Discussion & Analysis part of 10-Ks and 10-Qs. That is where companies review their performance and explain how they arrive at certain numbers. It's where retailers, for example, detail how they calculate comparable store sales, which is usually defined as stores open at least 12 months. According to a disclosure in its filings, however, men's clothing retailer Jos. A. Bank excludes stores that had competition from new Bank stores within ten miles of "their immediate market area over the prior 12 months." In response to investor questions about comp store sales on a recent conference call, CEO Robert Wildrick said, "Don't get hung up on comps. It is not the way professionals look at business." Maybe not, but it is the way investors look at retailers, and you'd know about the quirky way Bank does it only by reading the fine print. As is the case with insurance policies, it's there for a reason.

Fortune
June 23, 2003
Page 124

Questions for Consideration

1. In an annual report read the first or second footnote, usually titled "Significant Accounting Policies." Do you believe that it contains important information in a readable format. Why or why not?

2. What change(s) in footnotes would make them more attractive to readers and encourage them to read the footnotes?

Assignment 12
The Statement of Cash Flows

Name of your company _____

The purpose of this assignment is to understand the information presented on your company's statement of cash flows. This financial statement is the only one that is *not* based on accrual accounting. It is a simple report of how much cash flowed into the company and how much cash flowed out. You will compare and contrast your company's cash flows from operating, financing, and investing activities.

Completing the Assignment

1. Indicate with a check mark below whether your firm's statement of cash flows was prepared using the direct approach or the indirect approach.

   a. _____ *Direct approach.* If the first line under Operating Activities reads "Cash received from customers," or something similar, the direct approach is being used.

   b. _____ *Indirect approach.* If the first line under Operating Activities reads "Net income," or something similar, the indirect approach is being used.

2. Does the net "change in cash" (sometimes labeled change in cash and cash equivalents) as reported on the statement of cash flows match the change in cash balance reported on the comparative balance sheets for the most recent two year period? If no, indicate the amount of change.

   _____ Yes

   _____ No

   $ _____ Amount of change, if yes

Note
The linkage of an item on one financial statement to an item reported on a different financial statement is referred to as *financial statement articulation.*

---

3. Unless a firm issued significant amounts of equity or debt, e.g., stocks or bonds, during a year, operating activities should be the largest source of cash. If operating activities aren't generating a significant amount of cash from year to year, the firm may be headed for trouble. A company that is regularly generating cash from investing activities also may be headed for trouble, i.e., the company may be selling off assets to pay its bills.

   a. Prepare a summary of your firm's cash flows. There should be three years of data on the statement of cash flows. There may be additional years summarized in the Financial Highlights section. Report as many years as you can, but not more than six, in millions of dollars.

Category	Most Recent Year	Prior Years (label each column below)				
Operating activities	____	____	____	____	____	____
Investing activities	____	____	____	____	____	____
Financing activities	____	____	____	____	____	____
Net change in cash during year	____	____	____	____	____	____

   b. What do you conclude from the information above? Does the company appear to be generating a healthy cash flow from operations over the years or is it depending on cash from other sources to pay its bills? Discuss.

   > **Note**
   > If cash from operations is often negative, it is a particularly bad sign. It means that every day when the company opens for business some of its cash "leaks out."

   _____

   _____

   _____

   _____

   _____

   _____

   _____

   _____

   _____

   _____

_____

_____

_____

_____

_____

_____

_____

_____

_____

_____

_____

_____

_____

_____

4. Usually, a company's operating activities and financing activities supply cash
   for investing activities. Examine your company's investing activities.
   a. Determine the amounts of cash and fill in the blanks below in millions of
      dollars.

	Most Recent Year	Prior Years (label each column below)				
	____	____ ____	____	____	____	____
1) Cash generated (used) by operating activities **plus** financing activities	____	____ ____	____	____	____	____
2) Cash generated (used) by investing activities	____	____ ____	____	____	____	____

   3) Is the cash provided by operating activities and financing activities
      together roughly equal to the amount of cash consumed by investing
      activities in each year? Answer "yes" or "no" for each year. (More than
      one "no" may indicate that further inquiry into cash flow is necessary.)

      ____   ____   ____   ____   ____   ____

   b. Summarize your findings regarding 4.a. In general, is the _usual_ situation
      occurring for your firm during the years studied? Are cash outflows from
      investing activities being adequately covered by cash inflows from operating
      activities and financing activities? Discuss.

_____

_____

_____

_____

_____

_____

_____

_____

_____

_____

_____

Note

Three ratios often are computed to assess the cash flow results of a firm.

Cash-based return on assets ratio is the cash-based equivalent of the accrual-based return on assets. In each case, the intent is to compare the results of operations to the amount of assets used to generate that result.

$$\frac{\text{net cash flow from operating activities}}{\text{average total assets}*}$$

Cash flow to current maturities of long-term debt ratio is a coverage ratio which measures the number of times that this year's current maturities of long-term debt could have been repaid from cash generated by this year's operating activities.

$$\frac{\text{net cash flow from operating activities}}{\text{current maturities of long} \cdot \text{term debt}}$$

Cash used by investing activities to long-term assets ratio measures the rate at which long-term assets are being replaced. A high ratio indicates that the firm is not merely replacing assets but is growing. A low rate may indicate that the company is failing to replace long-term assets on a timely basis and faces a risk of obsolescence.

$$\frac{\text{cash used by investing activities}}{\text{average long} \cdot \text{term assets}*}$$

*   beginning total (long · term) assets   +   ending total (long · term assets)

2

5. Compute each of the ratios below for the most recent year for your firm.

   a. cash based return on assets $= \dfrac{\text{net cash flow from operating activities}}{\text{average total assets}}$

   cash based return on assets $= \underline{\hspace{10cm}} = \underline{\hspace{4cm}}$

   b. $\left(\begin{array}{c}\text{cash flow to current maturities}\\\text{of long} \cdot \text{term debt}\end{array}\right) = \dfrac{\text{net cash flow from operating activities}}{\text{current maturities of long} \cdot \text{term debt}}$

   $\left(\begin{array}{c}\text{cash flow to current maturities}\\\text{of long} \cdot \text{term debt}\end{array}\right) = \underline{\hspace{8cm}} = \underline{\hspace{4cm}}$

   c. $\left(\begin{array}{c}\text{cash used by investing activities}\\\text{to long} \cdot \text{term debt}\end{array}\right) = \dfrac{\text{cash used by investing activities}}{\text{average long} \cdot \text{term assets}}$

   $\left(\begin{array}{c}\text{cash used by investing activities}\\\text{to long} \cdot \text{term debt}\end{array}\right) = \underline{\hspace{8cm}} = \underline{\hspace{4cm}}$

6. To give perspective to the ratios computed above, check with five classmates to compare the value of the ratios for their firms to yours. Record the information below.

Alternative

As an alternative to comparing your company's values with those of your classmates' companies, you may want to compare with the companies you used in No. 3.e. of Assignment 3.

Check with your professor to make sure this option is acceptable.

	Your Firm	COMPARATIVE FIRMS				
		Firm 1	Firm 2	Firm 3	Firm 4	Firm 5
a. Cash-based return on assets	_____	_____	_____	_____	_____	_____
b. Cash flow to current maturities of long-term debt	_____	_____	_____	_____	_____	_____
c. Cash used by investing activities to long-term debt	_____	_____	_____	_____	_____	_____

7. How do your firm's cash-based ratios correlate to those of your comparative firms? Do some appear high? Some low? All about the same? Be specific.

   Is there anything about your firm, its industry, or your comparative companies or industries that would tend to explain the differences between your company's ratios and those of other firms? Discuss.

8. Did your firm report any significant *noncash* financing and investing activities (often called direct exchanges) for its most recent year? For example, issuing common stock (financing activity) to acquire land (investment activity) is normally considered a significant noncash financing and investing activity.

    Hint: *These usually are found at the bottom of the statement of cash flows or in a separate schedule that accompanies the statement of cash flows.*

    a. If yes, describe these transactions below. If no, write "none."

    _____

    _____

    _____

    _____

    _____

    _____

    _____

    _____

    _____

    _____

    _____

    _____

    b. For each item listed in 8.a. explain how the transaction affected your firm's balance sheet.

    _____

    _____

    _____

    _____

    _____

    _____

    _____

    _____

    _____

    _____

    _____

    _____

    _____

9. Now that you have studied your company's segment and cash flow information, you have all the information needed to further analyze your company.

Guide for Memo No. 4

a. Did you find the segment disclosures sufficient for you to gain a better understanding of your company? Are the reported segments consistent with what you thought your company would have as segments? Explain.

b. Over the three years of cash flow information found in your company's reported Statement of Cash Flows, has your company's cash position improved, weakened, or remained about the same? Explain.

Reading 12
Is That Revenue for Real?

By Andrew T. Gillies

When companies fudge their numbers, they usually start with the top line. But it's hard to fudge cash receipts, so keep an eye on the cash.

A little over a year ago Duke Energy declared it had finished its "best year ever," despite Enron's collapse and the other problems afflicting the energy business at the time. It reported revenue of $60 billion, by that measure making it the 13th-largest U.S. corporation.

But the "best year ever" didn't look so great the following June, when a task force at the Financial Accounting Standards Board reached a new consensus on how to account for energy trading. Reversing a position taken in 1998, it decreed that energy trades should be recorded on a net, not a gross, basis. In other words, if a company trades an energy futures contract for $100,000 and makes a $2,000 spread on the trade, it should recognize as revenue only the $2,000.

Whoosh. Duke Energy restated its revenues going back to 1997. With 2002 sales of $15 billion, the company ranks 115th on this year's Forbes Sales 500. The stock has fallen from $37 to $13 over the past year.

A lot of puffery has been going into the top line. According to the Huron Consulting Group, a Chicago firm focused on corporate finance and restructuring, revenue recognition problems were behind 85 of the 381 accounting restatements of public companies in 2002. Typical mischief: recording a sale without accounting for the fact that the buyer has the right to return the goods, or, worse, hasn't even taken title to them; counting revenue from deals with unfulfilled obligations (such as future consulting services).

In February the Securities & Exchange Commission filed fraud charges against eight past and present employees of Qwest Communications. The SEC says that, among other things, Qwest cooked up false internal documents to justify treating a $34 million equipment sale as something that could be booked in its June 2001 quarter. Qwest has overstated revenues in other ways, for example, by swapping fiber-optic capacity with other telecom companies. As of the latest tally the company had restated its 2001 revenues downward by $1.3 billion, or 7%.

From July 1997 to July 2002 the SEC launched 227 investigations of suspected financial misreporting, 126 of them relating to revenue recognition. Improper timing of sales is the biggest offense--borrowing from the next quarter in a desperate effort to make the analysts happy for this quarter. The SEC also found 80 cases of utterly fictitious revenues and 21 cases of improperly valued revenue, such as the right-of-return cases mentioned earlier.

To book a sale you need only two things, at least in theory: to deliver goods or services, and to have a reasonable expectation of payment. Business reality, however, is rarely that cut-and-dried. And don't expect last year's Sarbanes-Oxley Act to end the ambiguities. "Accounting is purposefully gray," says April Klein, a professor of accounting at New York University. "If you make too many rules, you won't be able to capture the individuality of the company."

In short, there will always be plenty of room for fudging, and some for outright chicanery. How to protect yourself as an investor? Spend as much time with the cash flow statement as with the profit-and-loss statement that precedes it. If a company is counting dubious transactions in its revenues, in all likelihood the buyers haven't paid yet, and so the cash flow from operations will be anemic in relation to reported profit. Look back at Enron's fiscal 1999 results, for instance, and you'll see growth in sales and net income of 27% but a 25% decrease in net cash from operations. It wasn't a good sign then; keep an eye out for it now.

Forbes
April 14, 2003
Page 161

Questions for Consideration

1. Why would managers increase revenue rather than reduce expenses to increase earnings?

2. Why is it better to look at the statement of cash flows rather than the income statement to assess a company's revenues?

Assignment 13
Capstone Project/Optional Final Memo

The purpose of this assignment is to integrate the information you have obtained about your company (or companies) and industry into a coordinated report. The report is to be typed and have a professional appearance. You should assume that your first post-college employer has asked you to research the firm you've been working on during this course. He/she may be considering your firm as a potential supplier, customer, competitor, or acquisition candidate. Your employer may even be secretly entertaining an offer of employment from this firm. Under any of these circumstances, you will want to present your employer with a carefully-researched, thoughtfully-written, and professionally-presented document.

Completing The Assignment

In general, unless modified by your professor, you have great flexibility in completing this assignment. For example, you may choose any organization structure for this report that you believe best captures and presents the necessary information. You should be creative and complete in your analyses and presentation. Generally, your report is to be based on the assignments you have completed during this course as part of the **Financial Reporting Project** (**FRP**). In some cases, however, you will want to include additional information or additional creative analysis that is especially important to understanding the financial health and status of your firm (or firms) and industry. Where appropriate, you should prepare charts or graphs to illustrate the facts you present.

Keep in mind that your employer may put your report to a variety of uses. For example:

▸ If your assigned firm is a prospective supplier, your employer would want to assess its long-run stability and its continuing ability to provide quality goods at reasonable prices.

▸ If your assigned firm is a potential customer, your employer will be concerned with its ability to meet its short-term obligations as they become due.

▸ If your assigned firm is a candidate for investment, your employer will want to understand its long-term financial structure, cost structure, and profit structure.

Your report should be flexible so that it can be used in any of these ways. Regardless of the format you use, your report must include a summary section that states your overall assessment of the financial health and status of your firm. For example, is it strong, weak, improving, or deteriorating? Would you make a short-term loan to this firm? Would you make a long-term loan to this firm? Would you buy stock or invest your career with this company? Discuss why or why not.

1. **Suggested Outline** – If you are unsure how to organize your report you might consider the following outline. It follows the assignment structure of the **FRP**.

   Important: *Be sure to check with your professor to determine if he/she has specific guidelines regarding the organization of your report.*

   a. Overview of the Industry

   b. Basic Company Information

   c. The Company's Economic, Social, Legal and Political Environment

   d. Overview of the Annual Report, SEC 10-K and Proxy Statement

   e. The Company's Independent Auditor

   f. The Income Statement

   g. Current Assets and Current Liabilities

   h. Long-term Assets and Long-term Liabilities

   i. Stockholders' Equity

   j. Segment Information

   k. The Cash Flow Statement

   l. Summary Statement on Financial Health and Status of the Company

   If you use this suggested outline, be careful that you don't merely make lists of the information that you collected on the assignment sheets of the **FRP**. The outline format of the assignments is very efficient for recording the data you found for your company, but it won't be very helpful to your employer. Remember, your employer hasn't read the articles or consulted the references that you have. You are expected to provide greater background, detail, analysis and commentary than what appears in your completed assignments.

2. **Due Date(s)** – To be announced by your professor.

3. **Annual Report**, **SEC 10-K**, and **Proxy Statement** – If you have not already done so, provide each of these documents to your professor when you turn in your report.

Note

If you are part of a team in which each member is researching a different firm, avoid the temptation to write a separate report for each company and staple the reports together. Instead, this report should be an *integrated* report in which the firms are compared, contrasted, and summarized in each section.

Your report must focus on comparisons and contrasts among the firms and on an integrated assessment of the overall industry situation. You are expected to provide greater background, detail, and analysis than what appears in your individual completed assignments.

---

4. Optional Memo No. 5 – Final Recommendation

If you have completed the first four memos, your professor may want you to prepare a final memo to complete the **FRP**.

Guide for Memo No. 5

a. Make your final recommendation to your client.

Briefly highlight significant information from previous memos to emphasize your point.

Include industry trends which could affect your company in the near future.

b. End your memo with a paragraph about the thoroughness of your firm in preparing information for your client and give one or two reasons why your new firm should continue to advise your client.

Reading 13
What if golfers used GAAP for keeping score?

By Paul B.W. Miller, Professor, University of Colorado and Paul R. Bahnson, Professor, Boise State University

THE SPIRIT OF ACCOUNTING

Over the last three years, Paul Miller has been living a double life – he's been both an accounting professor and the creator of a new undergraduate program in professional golf management at his school. As a result, he has been thinking more about the game than usual.

It was out of this ferment that he drew a connection between financial reporting and score keeping in golf that led to our publishing a column in July 2001. We have always considered it one of our better ones, and feedback confirms that others have enjoyed it, despite its sharp criticism of generally accepted accounting principles and those who create and implement it.

We offer it again for those who missed it or who may have forgotten its message.

For several reasons, we have been thinking about golf lately, and it's occurred to us that the game would be a lot different if players kept score using generally accepted accounting principles. Along those lines, we've imagined that a standard-setting agency for scoring might create principles for a "generally accepted golf scoring" system called GAGS.

Of course, one conspicuous difference would be that the scorecard would include 10 pages of footnotes.

Included in GAGS would be the practice of allocating a predicted number of putts per round among the holes expected to be played, all without regard to the actual number. For example, it might be common to allocate two putts to each hole. While this practice would eliminate all fear of the three-putt, it would also do away with one-putts and chip-ins, but that would be the price of eliminating both volatility and the risk associated with reporting what really happens.

Another GAGS principle would allow for off-scorecards-and-shots when certain criteria are met. Even though anyone could observe that a ball landed in the trap and that the golfer took several shots to get it onto the green, the rules would allow players to leave those strokes out simply because they didn't intend for the ball to wind up in the sand and didn't want to look bad.

Another popular feature of GAGS would be the deferral of strokes in excess of par. Under this system, players would record no score higher than par on any hole despite actually having a bogey, double bogey or worse. The excess strokes would simply be deferred without penalty until they could be offset against birdies or eagles that might be scored in rounds to be played in the future, if ever. Again, the goal would be to eliminate volatility by destroying any connection between the carded scores and actual results.

Another standard would apply the lower-of-past-or-present-score method. Under this practice, golfers would maintain records of the lowest score ever achieved on each hole. Then, during a real round, they would enter an actual score on a given hole only if it was lower than their previous low score.

One more feature of GAGS would include pairs of alternative practices, one preferable and the other merely acceptable.

For example, consider shots into water hazards. When players hit into the drink, they would have the option of adding that stroke plus a penalty to their score, or merely disclosing them in a footnote that shows the pro forma score computed as if the shots had actually been counted.

Now, try to imagine what would happen when golfers using GAGS tried to compete in tournaments with players who apply the strict rules of golf. Further, suppose that all spectators are aware of GAGS but only want to know the real number of strokes taken.

In these circumstances, wouldn't the prize money go to the players who have the fewest actual strokes, instead of those who merely report the smallest number?

It doesn't take much imagination to see the connections

between GAGS and GAAP:

♦ The really helpful information appears in the footnotes, not the financial statements.

♦ Instead of allocating putts equally among holes, accountants allocate depreciation equally among years without ever checking to see what happened to the asset's real value.

♦ Carefully crafted agreements allow lease liabilities to be left off the balance sheet.

♦ Lower-of-cost-or-market is still applied to inventories; even though it is no longer applied to investments, FASB requires managers to write down impaired assets but forbids writing up enhanced assets.

♦ The deferral method causes companies that actually pay income taxes to postpone reporting the expense until later years, if and when reported pre-tax income is higher. Both of us personally gag over the way undesired gains and losses for defined-benefit pension plans are deferred simply to avoid reporting the volatile truth.

♦ SFAS 123 allows managers to describe options-based compensation in pro forma footnotes instead of deducting it from reported earnings.

What's important to realize is that the capital market doesn't consist of ignorant or complacent spectators; instead, its sophisticated participants watch each public company carefully and develop their own scorecards based on actual events without believing the compromised, predicted, smoothed, deferred, and grossly incomplete and misleading numbers in GAAP reports.

The market's prize money goes to those who create greater future cash flow potential instead of those who fabricate the highest reported earnings.

This analogy shows that it is foolish to believe that GAAP statements even approximate actual results and conditions. Just as the winner in a strict rules tournament has the lowest number of actual strokes, winners in the capital market are managers who are most likely to achieve the highest real future earnings and cash flows.

Even if they report the occasional bad news with candor as soon as it happens, the gallery cheers them on, and they are still eligible to compete in the future. The only permanent losers are cheaters who are likely to be banished from competing at the highest level.

It's long past time for a change in outlook and practice. Because the standard-setting process is so compromised by political pressure and so characterized by ducking hard issues (like goodwill), financial statements don't reflect anything that really happens. The capital market knows it and stock prices reflect it. Smart managers should stop fooling themselves because they sure aren't fooling anyone else.

In closing, let's hear the hushed words of a TV commentator at the first tee for the final round of the British Open: "Fans, the championship is over. Lyon Forrest and Mel Michael-son have just compared their anticipated scores for today's rounds and Michaelson has won the tournament because his predicted score of 62 is lower than the 64 that Forrest expected to shoot. What an amazing turn of events and a great victory powered by one of the sport's greatest imaginations!"

Nonsense, but then so are most managers' GAAP earnings announcements.

Plus ça change

This column's first appearance predated Enron, et al, and the demise of Andersen. There is no denying that many accountants' and managers' imaginations definitely outran the truth.

The accounting reforms to date do not guarantee that financial scorecards will portray what is actually happening, and it is absurd to think that these or any other regulatory efforts can lead us to that goal.

The solution is for the players to understand that the game is real and that there are severe consequences for doctoring the score. The beauty of Quality Financial Reporting is that it shows that there are powerful financial rewards for counting all of the strokes. Some managers are getting the message but others are bound to be disappointed when they enter the capital market clubhouse with a scorecard that no one believes.

Accounting Today
August 4 - 17, 2003
Pages 14 and 16

Questions for Consideration

This reading is included to end the **FRP** on a light note. There are no questions.

Appendix A
Accounting Synonyms

One of the perplexing aspects of learning accounting is that there is so much variation in terminology. Often, two or more terms mean exactly (or very nearly) the same thing. If you don't recognize a particular term, look it up here. You may have already learned the concept or principle under a similar or different name.

Accounting Term
Alternative Accounting Terms

A

Accounting Term	Alternative Accounting Terms
Acid-Test Ratio	Quick Ratio
Accounting Equation	Basic Accounting Equation; Balance Sheet Equation
Accounting Rate of Return	Simple Rate of Return
Allowance for Bad Debts	Allowance for Doubtful Accounts; Allowance for Uncollectible Accounts
Allowance for Doubtful Accounts	Allowance for Bad Debts
Allowance for Uncollectible Accounts	Allowance for Bad Debts
Annuity	Ordinary Annuity
Asset	Unexpired Cost

B

Accounting Term	Alternative Accounting Terms
Bad Debts Expense	Uncollectible Accounts Expense
Balance Sheet	Statement of Financial Position; Statement of Financial Condition
Balance Sheet Equation	Accounting Equation; Basic Accounting Equation
Basic Accounting Equation	Accounting Equation; Balance Sheet Equation
Basket Purchase	Lump-sum Purchase (or acquisition); Joint Purchase; Group Purchase
Bearer Bond	Coupon Bond
Book of Original Entry	Journal; General Journal
Book Value	Carrying Value
Burden	Factory Burden; Overhead; Manufacturing Overhead
Business Entity Concept	Entity Concept; Separate Entity Concept

C

Accounting Term	Alternative Accounting Terms
Capital Stock	generic term for either common or preferred stock
Carrying Value	Book Value
Cash Discount	either a Sales Discount or Purchase Discount, depending on the circumstances
Cash Value	Fair Value; Fair Market Value; Market Value
Cash Equivalent Value	same as Cash Value
Charge an account	Debit an Account
Closely Held Corporation	Nonpublic Corporation
Common Stock	Capital Stock
Constant-Dollar Accounting	Price-Level Accounting; GPL Accounting
Contract (Interest) Rate	Stated Rate; Coupon Rate; Nominal Rate; Face Rate
Continuity Principle	Going Concern Principle
Contributed Capital	Paid-In Capital
Contribution Approach to Pricing	Variable Approach to Pricing

Coupon Bond	Bearer Bond
Coupon (Interest) Rate	Stated Rate; Nominal Rate; Face Rate; Contract Rate
Current Cost Accounting	Current Value Accounting
Current Ratio	Working Capital Ratio
Current Value Accounting	Current Cost Accounting

D

Debenture Bond	Unsecured Bond
Differential Cost	Incremental Cost
Direct Costing	Variable Costing
Direct Labor Efficiency Variance	Labor Efficiency Variance; Labor Usage Variance; Direct Labor Usage Variance
Direct Labor Price Variance	Direct Labor Rate Variance
Direct Labor Rate Variance	Labor Price Variance; Direct Labor Price Variance; Labor Rate Variance
Direct Labor Usage Variance	Direct Labor Efficiency Variance
Direct Materials Quantity Variance	Materials Quantity Variance; Materials Usage Variance; Direct Materials Usage Variance;
Direct Materials Usage Variance	Direct Materials Quantity Variance

E

Earnings	Income; Profit
Earnings Statement	Income Statement; Profit and Loss Statement
Effective Interest Rate	Market Rate; Yield Rate
Entity Principle (or concept)	Separate Entity Principle (or concept); Business Entity Principle (or concept)
Expense	Expired Cost
Expense and Revenue Summary account	Income Summary account
Expired Cost	Expense

F

Face (Interest) Rate	Stated Rate; Coupon Rate; Nominal Rate; Contract Rate
Face Value (of bonds or notes)	Par Value; Maturity Value; Principal
Factory Burden	Burden; Overhead; Manufacturing Overhead
Fair Market Value	Fair Value; Cash Value; Market Value
Fair Value	Fair Market Value; Cash Value; Market Value
Financial Leverage	Leverage; Trading on the Equity
Fixed Assets	Plant Assets; Productive Assets; Tangible Assets; Property, Plant and Equipment
Freight-In	Transportation-In

G

Going Concern Principle	Continuity Principle
General Journal	Journal; Book of Original Entry
General Price-Level Accounting	Price-Level Accounting; Constant-Dollar Accounting; GPL Accounting
General Price-Level Gain/Loss	Price-Level Gain/Loss
GPL Accounting	General Price-Level Accounting; Price-Level Accounting; Constant-Dollar Accounting
Gross Margin (on sales)	Gross Profit
Gross Profit (on sales)	Gross Margin
Group Purchase	Basket Purchase; Lump-sum Purchase; Joint Purchase

H

High Yield Bond	Junk Bond; Speculative Grade Bond
Hurdle Rate	Minimum Desired Rate (of return)

I

Income	Earnings; Profit
Income Statement	Earnings Statement; Profit and Loss Statement
Income Summary account	Expense and Revenue Summary account
Incremental Cost	Differential Cost
Internal Rate of Return	Time Adjusted Rate of Return
Inventory	Merchandise Inventory

J

Joint Purchase	Basket Purchase; Lump-sum Purchase; Group Purchase
Journal	General Journal; Book of Original Entry
Junk Bond	High Yield Bond; Speculative Grade Bond

L

Labor Efficiency Variance	Direct Labor Efficiency Variance
Labor Price Variance	Direct Labor Price Variance
Labor Rate Variance	Direct Labor Rate Variance
Labor Usage Variance	Direct Labor Efficiency Variance
Leverage	Financial Leverage; Trading on the Equity
Lump-Sum Purchase	Basket Purchase (or acquisition); Joint Purchase; Group Purchase

M

Manufacturing Overhead	Overhead; Burden; Factory Burden
Marketable Securities	Temporary Investments; Short-term Investments
Market (Interest) Rate	Effective Rate; Yield Rate
Market Value	Fair Value; Fair Market Value; Cash Value; Current Value
Materials Quantity Variance	Direct Materials Quantity Variance
Materials Usage Variance	Direct Materials Usage Variance
Maturity Value (of bonds)	Face Value; Principal; Par Value
Merchandise Inventory	Inventory
Minimum Desired Rate (of return)	Hurdle Rate
Monetary Unit Principle	Unit-of-Measure Principle
Mortgage Bond	Secured Bond

N

Net Earnings	Net Income; Net Profit
Net Income	Net Profit; Net Earnings
Net Profit	Net Income; Net Earnings
Nominal Account	Temporary Account
Nominal (Interest) Rate	Stated Rate; Coupon Rate; Face Rate; Contract Rate
Nonpublic Corporation	Closely Held Corporation
Normal Operating Cycle	Operating Cycle

O

Operating Cycle	Normal Operating Cycle
Ordinary Annuity	Annuity
Ordinary Bonds	Term Bonds

Overhead	Manufacturing Overhead; Burden; Factory Burden
Owners' Equity	Shareholders' Equity; Stockholders' Equity

P

Paid-In Capital	Contributed Capital
Partnership Agreement	Partnership Contract; Articles of Co-Partnership
Par Value (of bonds)	Face Value; Principal; Maturity Value
Periodicity Principle	Time-Period Principle
Permanent Account	Real Account
Plant Assets	Fixed Assets; Property, Plant and Equipment; Productive Assets; Tangible Assets
Preferred Stock	Capital Stock
Price-Level Accounting	Constant-Dollar Accounting; GPL Accounting; General Price-Level Accounting;
Price-Level Gain/Loss	General Price-Level Gain/Loss
Principal (of bonds)	Face Value; Maturity Value; Par Value
Productive Assets	Plant Assets; Property, Plant and Equipment; Fixed Assets; Tangible Assets
Profit	Income; Earnings
Profit and Loss Statement	Income Statement; Earnings Statement
Property, Plant and Equipment	Plant Assets; Fixed Assets; Productive Assets; Tangible Assets
Purchase Discount	Cash Discount

Q

Quick Ratio	Acid-Test Ratio

R

Real Account	Permanent Account

S

Sales Discount	Cash Discount
Secured Bond	Mortgage Bond
Separate Entity Principle	Entity Principle (or concept); Business Entity Principle
Shareholders' Equity	Stockholders' Equity; Owners' Equity
Short-term Investments	Temporary Investments; Marketable Securities
Simple Rate of Return	Accounting Rate of Return
Speculative Grade Bond	Junk Bond; High Yield Bond
Stated (Interest) Rate	Coupon Rate; Face Rate; Nominal Rate; Contract Rate
Statement of Financial Condition	Balance Sheet; Statement of Financial Position
Statement of Financial Position	Balance Sheet; Statement of Financial Condition
Stockholders' Equity	Shareholders' Equity; Owners' Equity

T

Tangible Assets	Fixed Assets; Plant Assets; Productive Assets; Property, Plant and Equipment
Tax Avoidance	Tax Planning
Tax Planning	Tax Avoidance
Temporary Account	Nominal Account
Temporary Investments	Short-term Investments; Marketable Securities
Term Bonds	Ordinary Bonds
Time Adjusted Rate of Return	Internal Rate of Return
Time-Period Principle	Periodicity Principle

Trading on the Equity   Leverage; Financial Leverage
Transportation-In   Freight-In

U
Uncollectible Accounts Expense   Bad Debts Expense
Unexpired Cost   Asset
Unit-of-Measure Principle   Monetary Unit Principle
Unsecured Bond   Debenture Bond

V
Variable Approach to Pricing   Contribution Approach to Pricing
Variable Costing   Direct Costing

W
Working Capital Ratio   Current Ratio

Y
Yield (Interest) Rate   Market Rate; Effective Rate

Appendix B
Common Acronyms

While reading annual reports, particularly in the notes, you may find acronyms with which you are not familiar. The acronyms most commonly found in annual reports are listed here.

Acronym	Identification
AICPA	American Institute of Certified Public Accountants
AMEX	American Stock Exchange
CEO	Chief Executive Officer
CFO	Chief Financial Officer
COO	Chief Operating Officer
CPA	Certified Public Accountant
EBIT	Earnings Before Interest and Taxes
EBITDA	Earnings Before Interest, Taxes, Depreciation and Amortization
EITF	Emerging Issues Task Force
EPS	Earnings Per Share
ESOP	Employee Stock Option Plan
FAS	Financial Accounting Standard
FASB	Financial Accounting Standards Board
FIFO	First-in, First-out
FSP	FASB Staff Positions
GAAP	Generally Accepted Accounting Principles
GAAS	Generally Accepted Auditing Standards
GASB	Government Accounting Standards Board
IAS	International Accounting Standard
IASB	International Accounting Standards Board
IFRS	International Financial Reporting Standards
IT	Information Technology
LCM	Lower-of-Cost-or-Market
LIFO	Last-in, First-out
LLC	Limited Liability Company
LLP	Limited Liability Partnership
MD&A	Management Discussion and Analysis
NASDAQ	National Association of Securities Dealers Automated Quotation
NYSE	New York Stock Exchange
PE	Price Earnings Ratio
PV	Present Value
PVFP	Present Value of Future Payments
R&D	Research and Development
ROE	Return on Equity
ROI	Return on Investment
S&P	Standard and Poors
SAB	Staff (SEC) Accounting Bulletin
SARs	Stock Appreciation Rights
SEC	Securities and Exchange Commission
SFAS	Statement of Financial Accounting Standard
SOP	Statement of Position
SPE	Special Purpose Entity

Appendix C
Summary of Ratios

Ratios vary from analyst to analyst. These commonly used versions, listed by assignment, appear in the *Financial Reporting Project*.

Ratio	Formula	Measures
Assignment 6 – Income Statement		
Earnings per share	$\dfrac{\text{net income}}{\text{number of common shares outstanding}}$	earnings per share of common stock
Gross profit margin	$\dfrac{\text{gross margin}}{\text{sales revenue}}$	efficiency in production or purchase of goods for sale
Net profit margin	$\dfrac{\text{net income}}{\text{sales revenue}}$	the ability to produce profits from sales
Operating profit margin	$\dfrac{\text{operating income}}{\text{sales revenue}}$	efficiency of the company's primary, or central, activities
Return on assets	$\dfrac{\text{net income}}{\text{average total assets}}$	the ability to generate profit from the investment in assets
Return on equity	$\dfrac{\text{net income}}{\text{average stockholders' equity}}$	return earned on capital invested by the firm's common stockholders
Assignment 7 – Current Assets and Current Liabilities		
Accounts receivable turnover	$\dfrac{\text{sales revenue}}{\text{average accounts receivable}}$	the ability to convert revenues to cash
Current ratio	$\dfrac{\text{current assets}}{\text{current liabilities}}$	the ability to pay off current obligations as they come due
Inventory turnover	$\dfrac{\text{cost of goods sold}}{\text{average inventory}}$	success in selling inventory
Quick (acid-test) ratio	$\dfrac{\text{cash} + \text{cash equivalent} + \text{short} \cdot \text{term invest.} + \text{A/R}}{\text{current liabilities}}$	the ability to pay short-term obligations from liquid current assets
Assignment 8 – Long-term Assets		
Depreciation and amortization to average long-term assets	$\dfrac{\text{depreciation expense} + \text{amortization expense}}{\text{average long} \cdot \text{term assets}}$	how rapidly the firm is writing off its long-term assets

Long-term assets to total assets	$\dfrac{\text{long} \cdot \text{term assets}}{\text{total assets}}$	financial flexibility
Plant assets to total assets	$\dfrac{\text{plant assets}}{\text{total assets}}$	financial flexibility focusing only on property, plant and equipment
Sales to average plant assets	$\dfrac{\text{sales}}{\text{average plant assets}}$	productivity of plant assets

Assignment 9 – Long-term Liabilities

Debt to total assets	$\dfrac{\text{total liabilities}}{\text{total assets}}$	the portion of assets that are provided by long-term creditors
Times interest earned	$\dfrac{\text{net income} + [\text{interest expense} (1 - \text{tax rate})]}{\text{interest expense}}$	the ability to pay annual interest charges on debt

Assignment 10 – Stockholders' Equity

Dividend payout	$\dfrac{\text{total cash dividends paid on common stock}}{\text{net income} - \text{preferred dividends}}$	the portion of net income distributed to stockholders in the form of dividends
Dividend yield	$\dfrac{\text{cash dividend per share of common stock}}{\text{market price per share of common stock}}$	cash return per share of common stock
Price-earnings (P/E)	$\dfrac{\text{current market price of common stock}}{\text{diluted earnings per share}}$	investors' expectations about a company's future earnings

Assignment 11 – Segment Information

Segment asset turnover	$\dfrac{\text{total segment revenues}}{\text{segment assets}}$	the ability of segment assets to generate segment revenues
Segment profit margin	$\dfrac{\text{segment profit}}{\text{total segment revenues}}$	the ability to produce segment profit from segment revenues

Assignment 12 – The Statement of Cash Flows

Cash-based return on assets	$\dfrac{\text{net cash flow from operating activities}}{\text{average total assets}}$	the ability to generate cash from operations from investment in assets
Cash flow to current maturities of long-term debt	$\dfrac{\text{net cash flow from operating activities}}{\text{current maturities of long} \cdot \text{term debt}}$	number of times current maturities of long-term debt could have been repaid from operating cash flows
Cash used by investing activities to long-term assets	$\dfrac{\text{cash used by investing activities}}{\text{average long} \cdot \text{term assets}}$	the rate at which long-term assets are being replaced